Table Of Contents

Chapter 1: Introduction to Podcasting

The Rise of Podcasting in 2024

In recent years, podcasting has emerged as a powerful medium for entrepreneurs, business professionals, music enthusiasts, sports professionals, and individuals from various backgrounds to share their knowledge, experiences, and stories with a global audience. As we look ahead to 2024, it is clear that podcasting will continue to rise and become an even more integral part of our daily lives.

For entrepreneurs and business professionals, podcasting offers a unique platform to showcase their expertise, share insights, and connect with a wider audience. With the increasing popularity of entrepreneurship, starting a podcast in 2024 will serve as a valuable tool to build a personal brand, network with industry leaders, and attract potential clients or investors.

Similarly, individuals interested in personal development and self-improvement will find an abundance of inspiring and educational podcasts tailored to their needs. With topics ranging from mindfulness and productivity to goal-setting and motivation, these podcasts will provide valuable guidance and support for those looking to enhance their personal and professional lives.

Health and wellness podcasts will also witness a significant surge in 2024. As individuals become increasingly conscious of their physical and mental well-being, podcasts focused on nutrition, fitness, mental health, and holistic healing will play a crucial role in providing expert advice, actionable tips, and inspirational stories to help listeners lead healthier lives.

Technology and innovation enthusiasts will have access to an array of podcasts that explore the latest trends, breakthroughs, and future possibilities. From artificial intelligence and blockchain to virtual reality and space exploration, these podcasts will keep listeners informed and inspired by the rapid advancements in various industries.

On the lighter side, comedy and entertainment podcasts will continue to bring joy and laughter to millions of listeners worldwide. With a diverse range of content, including stand-up comedy, storytelling, and celebrity interviews, these podcasts will serve as a source of entertainment and relaxation for individuals seeking a break from their busy lives.

For avid travelers and adventure enthusiasts, podcasts will offer a gateway to the world. Whether it's exploring new destinations, learning about different cultures, or gaining insights from experienced travelers, these podcasts will fuel wanderlust and inspire unforgettable adventures.

Lastly, sports enthusiasts will have access to an extensive range of podcasts covering their favorite sports, athletes, and teams. From in-depth analysis and game predictions to inspiring stories and interviews, these podcasts will keep fans engaged and connected to the world of sports.

In conclusion, podcasting is set to experience a meteoric rise in 2024, offering a plethora of opportunities for entrepreneurs, business professionals, music enthusiasts, sports professionals, and individuals seeking personal growth, entertainment, and inspiration. With the power to educate, entertain, and connect people across the globe, podcasts will undoubtedly become an essential part of our daily routines in the years to come.

Understanding the Power of Podcasting

In recent years, the world of podcasting has exploded in popularity. With millions of people tuning in to their favorite shows on a regular basis, it has become an incredibly powerful tool for entrepreneurs, business professionals, musicians, film graduates, and sports enthusiasts alike. In this subchapter, we will delve into the various ways in which podcasting can be a game-changer for individuals in different niches.

For entrepreneurs and business professionals, podcasting offers a unique platform to reach a wide audience and establish themselves as industry experts. By sharing valuable insights, tips, and advice, they can attract potential clients, build brand credibility, and ultimately, drive business growth. Moreover, podcasts provide an opportunity to network with other professionals in the field, potentially leading to exciting collaborations and partnerships.

For musicians and film professionals, podcasting opens up new avenues to showcase their talent and connect with fans. By discussing their creative process, sharing stories from their journey, and even featuring their music or film projects, they can cultivate a loyal following and expand their reach beyond traditional channels. Additionally, podcasting allows for collaborations with other artists, creating a vibrant community of like-minded individuals.

Sports enthusiasts can also benefit greatly from podcasting. By hosting shows that delve into the latest sports news, analysis, and interviews with athletes and experts, they can provide valuable content to fellow enthusiasts. This not only helps to foster a sense of community but can also lead to opportunities such as sponsorships, partnerships, and even media coverage.

Podcasting is not limited to specific industries or niches; it caters to a wide range of interests. For those interested in personal development and self-improvement, podcasts offer a wealth of knowledge and inspiration. Whether it's exploring topics such as mindfulness, goal-setting, or career advancement, these shows can be a valuable resource for individuals seeking personal growth.

Health and wellness podcasts are another popular genre. From fitness tips to mental health discussions, these shows provide listeners with practical advice and motivation to lead healthier lives. With an increasing focus on well-being, these podcasts can attract a dedicated and engaged audience.

Technology and innovation podcasts are perfect for tech enthusiasts. They offer in-depth discussions on the latest advancements, industry trends, and insights from experts. These shows serve as a platform for entrepreneurs and professionals to stay up-to-date with the rapidly evolving tech landscape.

Comedy and entertainment podcasts provide a much-needed escape from everyday life. With hilarious banter, storytelling, and interviews with comedians, these shows offer a laughter-filled experience for listeners. They are a perfect choice for those seeking light-hearted entertainment.

For those with a passion for travel and adventure, podcasts can transport them to exotic locations and provide insider tips from experienced travelers. From exciting travel stories to travel hacks, these shows are a great source of inspiration for the wanderlust-filled souls.

Lastly, sports enthusiasts can find a plethora of podcasts dedicated to their favorite teams, sports news, and analysis. These shows offer a platform for fans to stay connected, share their opinions, and engage in lively discussions about their favorite sports.

In conclusion, podcasting has become a powerful medium that caters to a diverse range of interests and industries. Whether you are an entrepreneur, business professional, musician, film graduate, or sports enthusiast, there is immense potential for growth and success through podcasting. By understanding the power of podcasting and leveraging its unique features, individuals can establish themselves as authorities, connect with their audience, and create a thriving community around their passion.

Benefits of Starting Your Own Podcast

In today's digital age, starting your own podcast can be a game-changer for entrepreneurs, business professionals, music professionals, sports enthusiasts, musicians, film graduates, and professionals alike. Whether you're looking to expand your audience, share your expertise, or simply have a creative outlet, podcasting offers numerous benefits that can propel your career or passion to new heights. Here are some compelling reasons why starting your own podcast in 2024 can be a game-changer for you:

1. Amplify your reach: Podcasting allows you to reach a global audience, connecting with people who share your interests or niche. It's an effective way to extend your brand, build credibility, and attract new opportunities.

2. Establish thought leadership: Hosting a podcast positions you as an expert in your field. By sharing valuable insights, interviewing industry leaders, and discussing relevant topics, you become a go-to resource for your audience. This can open doors for speaking engagements, partnerships, and collaborations.

3. Personal development and self-improvement: Podcasting can be a transformative journey for both the host and the audience. Through thoughtful conversations, you can explore personal development, self-improvement, and inspire others to do the same. It's a platform to share knowledge, experiences, and techniques that can positively impact lives.

4. Health and wellness promotion: If you're passionate about health and wellness, starting a podcast focused on this niche can be incredibly rewarding. You can educate, motivate, and inspire your audience to prioritize their well-being, share tips for a healthy lifestyle, and interview experts in the field.

5. Technology and innovation insights: Podcasts centered around technology and innovation are in high demand. This niche allows you to discuss emerging trends, review new products, and share insights into the world of technology. It's an opportunity to bridge the gap between tech enthusiasts and industry professionals.

6. Comedy and entertainment: Laughter is the best medicine, and comedy and entertainment podcasts are thriving in today's fast-paced world. If you have a knack for humor and storytelling, starting a podcast in this genre can bring joy to your audience and create a loyal following.

7. Travel and adventure exploration: Podcasts about travel and adventure allow you to transport your listeners to far-off places and inspire their wanderlust. Share stories, tips, and hidden gems from your own travels, or interview globetrotters and adventurers who can provide unique perspectives.

8. Sports enthusiasts' haven: For sports enthusiasts, podcasting offers a platform to discuss their favorite teams, athletes, and sports events. You can provide analysis, insights, and engage in lively discussions about the sports world, attracting a passionate fan base.

In conclusion, starting your own podcast in 2024 can be a game-changer, regardless of your niche. Whether you aim to educate, entertain, or inspire, podcasting offers a unique opportunity to connect with an audience, establish thought leadership, and pursue your passions. So, grab your microphone, unleash your creativity, and embark on an exciting podcasting journey that can transform your personal and professional life.

Chapter 2: Getting Started

Identifying Your Niche and Target Audience

In the ever-evolving world of podcasting, finding your niche and target audience is crucial to standing out from the crowd and creating a successful podcast. Whether you are an aspiring entrepreneur, a business professional, a music enthusiast, or a sports professional, understanding your niche and target audience will help you create content that resonates with your listeners and keeps them coming back for more.

Start by asking yourself, "What is my passion and expertise?" This is the foundation of your niche. If you are an entrepreneur, consider starting a podcast in 2024 that focuses on the challenges and triumphs of starting your own business. Share your experiences, interview other successful entrepreneurs, and provide valuable insight into the world of entrepreneurship. Your target audience, in this case, would be aspiring entrepreneurs who are looking for guidance and inspiration.

If you are interested in personal development and self-improvement, consider starting a podcast that offers practical advice, tips, and strategies for personal growth. Dive deep into topics such as mindset, goal-setting, time management, and success habits. Your target audience would be individuals who are seeking to improve their lives and reach their full potential.

Health and wellness are topics that resonate with a wide range of people. Consider starting a podcast that explores various aspects of health, fitness, nutrition, and mental well-being. Interview experts in the field, share personal stories, and provide practical tips for living a healthier and happier life. Your target audience would be individuals who are passionate about their well-being and are actively seeking information and inspiration in this area.

Technology and innovation are rapidly changing industries, making them perfect niches for a podcast. If you're a tech enthusiast, consider starting a podcast that delves into the latest trends, inventions, and breakthroughs in technology. Discuss the impact of technology on various industries and interview experts in the field. Your target audience would be individuals who are fascinated by the ever-evolving world of technology and want to stay up-to-date with the latest developments.

If you have a knack for making people laugh or entertaining others, consider starting a comedy and entertainment podcast. Share funny stories, interview comedians, and discuss the latest trends in the entertainment industry. Your target audience would be individuals who are looking for a lighthearted escape and enjoy being entertained.

For sports enthusiasts, starting a podcast that focuses on their favorite sports or teams can be a great way to connect with like-minded individuals. Discuss the latest games, analyze strategies, and interview sports professionals. Your target audience would be individuals who are passionate about sports and want to stay informed and engaged.

These are just a few examples of the many niches and target audiences you can explore when starting your own podcast. Remember, the key is to find a niche that aligns with your passion and expertise and identify a target audience that is eager to consume the content you create. By doing so, you will be on your way to creating a podcast that stands out in the crowded podcasting landscape of 2024.

Choosing a Podcast Format

When starting your own podcast, one of the most important decisions you'll make is choosing the right format for your show. The format you choose will set the tone and structure of your podcast, and it's crucial to select one that aligns with your goals and resonates with your target audience. In this subchapter, we will explore various podcast formats that cater to different niches and discuss how each format can be leveraged to create engaging and successful podcasts.

For entrepreneurs and business professionals, interview-style podcasts can be highly effective. This format allows you to invite industry experts and thought leaders as guests, providing valuable insights and expertise to your audience. It also helps to build credibility and establish yourself as a knowledgeable host in your field.

Podcasts focused on personal development and self-improvement thrive on storytelling and narrative-based formats. Sharing personal experiences, success stories, and actionable tips can inspire and motivate listeners to make positive changes in their lives. Incorporating interviews with experts in the field can bring a fresh perspective and further enhance the value of your podcast.

Health and wellness podcasts can benefit from a conversational format, where hosts engage in discussions about various health topics, share advice, and answer audience questions. This format creates a sense of community and encourages listeners to participate by submitting their queries or sharing their own experiences.

Technology and innovation podcasts can adopt a news-style format, where hosts discuss the latest trends, breakthroughs, and advancements in the tech world. Including interviews with industry leaders and experts can provide valuable insights and keep your audience informed about the ever-evolving tech landscape.

For those looking to entertain, comedy and entertainment podcasts are a great choice. This format allows hosts to bring humor, storytelling, and engaging banter to the forefront. Incorporating skits, interviews with comedians, and exploring pop culture can keep your listeners entertained and coming back for more.

Podcasts about travel and adventure can adopt a documentary-style format. Sharing personal travel experiences, interviewing globetrotters, and discussing various destinations can transport listeners to different parts of the world and ignite their wanderlust.

Sports enthusiasts can enjoy podcasts that adopt a commentary-style format, where hosts discuss recent sports events, analyze games, and offer their insights. Including interviews with athletes, coaches, and sports professionals can provide listeners with unique perspectives and behind-the-scenes stories.

In conclusion, choosing the right podcast format is crucial to the success of your show. Whether you aim to start a podcast in 2024, cater to aspiring entrepreneurs, focus on personal development, health and wellness, technology and innovation, comedy and entertainment, travel and adventure, or sports enthusiasts, selecting a format that aligns with your niche and audience is key. Consider the objectives of your podcast and the preferences of your target listeners to create a format that engages, educates, and entertains.

Equipment and Software Requirements

In order to embark on your podcasting journey and create high-quality content, it is crucial to have the right equipment and software. This subchapter will guide you through the essential tools needed to start your own podcast in 2024 and cater to various niches such as personal development, health and wellness, technology, comedy, travel, and sports.

First and foremost, you will need a reliable microphone to ensure crystal-clear audio. For entrepreneurs and business professionals, a USB condenser microphone like the Blue Yeti is recommended for its versatility and ease of use. Musicians and film graduates, on the other hand, might prefer a studio-grade XLR microphone such as the Audio-Technica AT2020 to capture professional-level sound.

To complement your microphone, you will require a pair of headphones for monitoring and editing your recordings. Sennheiser HD 280 Pro headphones are highly recommended for their excellent sound quality and noise isolation. These headphones are ideal for music professionals, film professionals, and sports enthusiasts looking to capture every detail of their recordings.

In terms of software, a digital audio workstation (DAW) is essential for editing and post-production. GarageBand, a free software for Mac users, is a popular choice for beginners due to its user-friendly interface and robust editing capabilities. For PC users, Adobe Audition offers a comprehensive set of tools and advanced features, making it ideal for professionals in the music and film industry.

Additionally, podcasters can enhance their recordings and create a more immersive experience by incorporating sound effects, intro/outro music, and jingles. Websites like AudioJungle and Epidemic Sound offer a wide range of royalty-free music and sound effects that can add a professional touch to your podcast.

Lastly, it is crucial to have a reliable hosting platform to distribute your podcast to various listening platforms such as Apple Podcasts, Spotify, and Google Podcasts. Platforms like Libsyn, Buzzsprout, and Anchor provide easy-to-use interfaces and analytics to track your podcast's performance and audience engagement.

Whether you are an aspiring entrepreneur, a sports enthusiast, or a health and wellness advocate, having the right equipment and software is crucial for launching a successful podcast. By investing in quality microphones, headphones, software, and hosting platforms, you can ensure that your podcast stands out in the crowded podcasting landscape of 2024.

Setting Up Your Recording Space

Creating a professional and functional recording space is essential for starting your own podcast. Whether you're a seasoned entrepreneur, a music professional, or a sports enthusiast looking to share your knowledge and passion with the world, having a well-equipped recording space can elevate the quality of your podcast and enhance the overall listening experience. In this subchapter, we will guide you through the process of setting up your recording space, ensuring that you have everything you need to produce high-quality content.

First and foremost, consider the location of your recording space. Choose a quiet room or area where you can minimize background noise and distractions. This will help you maintain a clean and professional sound throughout your episodes. If possible, opt for a space with good acoustics and minimal echo, as this will further enhance the audio quality.

Next, invest in the right equipment. Start with a reliable microphone that suits your needs and budget. There are various options available in the market, ranging from entry-level to professional-grade microphones. Consider your niche and target audience when selecting the microphone, as different microphones are better suited for specific types of podcasts.

Additionally, you'll need a pair of headphones to monitor your audio while recording. This will allow you to catch any sound issues or inconsistencies in real-time. Look for closed-back headphones that provide good isolation, ensuring that the audio from your playback doesn't bleed into your microphone.

To improve the acoustics of your recording space, consider adding soundproofing materials such as acoustic foam or panels. These can help reduce echoes and unwanted background noise, resulting in a cleaner sound.

Furthermore, don't forget about the importance of proper lighting. Ensure that your recording space is well-lit, either with natural light or artificial lighting. This will not only enhance the visual appeal of any video recordings but also create a more professional atmosphere.

Finally, organize your space in a way that promotes efficiency and comfort. Invest in a sturdy desk or table to hold your equipment, and consider using a microphone arm or stand to free up your hands during recording. Keep your cables and accessories neatly organized to avoid any unnecessary distractions.

By following these guidelines, you'll be well on your way to creating a professional recording space that meets the specific needs of your podcast. Remember, a well-equipped recording space contributes to the overall quality and success of your podcast, attracting and retaining listeners from all walks of life.

Chapter 3: Planning Your Podcast

Defining Your Podcast's Purpose and Goals

When embarking on the journey of starting your own podcast, it is crucial to define its purpose and goals right from the beginning. This subchapter will guide you through the process of understanding the importance of a clear vision for your podcast and help you tailor it to resonate with your target audience.

For entrepreneurs and business professionals, podcasts have become a powerful tool for sharing knowledge, insights, and experiences. By starting a podcast in 2024, you can position yourself as an industry expert, offering valuable advice and strategies to aspiring entrepreneurs. Craft your podcast's purpose around providing practical tips, success stories, and interviews with influential figures to inspire and empower your listeners.

Personal development and self-improvement are popular topics for podcasts, attracting an audience seeking motivation and guidance. By focusing your podcast on these themes, you can help individuals unleash their full potential, improve their mindset, and achieve personal growth. Share stories of personal triumphs, offer practical exercises, and interview experts in the field to create a podcast that sparks positive change in people's lives.

Health and wellness podcasts have seen a surge in popularity, with listeners seeking advice on nutrition, fitness, mental health, and overall well-being. Tailor your podcast to address these topics, providing expert advice, tips for healthy living, and interviews with healthcare professionals. Empower your audience to take charge of their health and make informed decisions.

In a rapidly evolving technological landscape, innovation and technology-focused podcasts are in high demand. Dive into the world of cutting-edge advancements, discuss emerging trends, and interview industry leaders to keep your audience informed and inspired. This niche attracts tech enthusiasts and professionals hungry for knowledge and insights.

For those seeking entertainment, comedy, and light-hearted content, a podcast centered around comedy and entertainment can be a great choice. Share funny stories, perform comedic skits, and interview popular comedians to create a podcast that brings joy and laughter to your audience's lives.

Travel and adventure podcasts are perfect for wanderlust-filled individuals who seek inspiration and information about exploring the world. Share travel stories, offer destination guides, and interview adventurers to transport your listeners to breathtaking locations and ignite their sense of wanderlust.

Lastly, sports enthusiasts crave content that covers their favorite teams, athletes, and the latest sporting events. Create a podcast that delves into the world of sports, providing analysis, interviews, and behind-the-scenes stories that keep your audience engaged and informed.

By defining your podcast's purpose and goals, you can attract the right audience and deliver content that meets their specific needs and interests. Tailor your podcast to one of these niches, understanding the unique desires of entrepreneurs, business professionals, music professionals, sports enthusiasts, musicians, film graduates, film professionals, and other target demographics. With a clear vision in mind, you can embark on your podcasting journey with confidence and purpose.

Creating Engaging Content Ideas

In order to create a successful podcast, it is crucial to have engaging content that captures the attention of your audience. In this subchapter, we will explore various strategies and techniques to generate compelling content ideas for your podcast.

1. Know Your Audience: Understanding your target audience is the first step in creating engaging content. Entrepreneurs, business professionals, music professionals, sports enthusiasts, musicians, film graduates, and professionals all have different interests and needs. Consider their preferences, pain points, and goals to develop content that resonates with them.

2. Brainstorming Sessions: Organize brainstorming sessions with your team or individually to generate content ideas. Encourage creativity and think outside the box. Consider topics related to starting a podcast in 2024, podcasts for aspiring entrepreneurs, personal development and self-improvement, health and wellness, technology and innovation, comedy and entertainment, travel and adventure, and sports enthusiasts.

3. Research and Trends: Stay updated with the latest trends and research in your niche. Read industry blogs, follow social media influencers, and listen to other podcasts in your field. This will help you identify popular topics, emerging trends, and gaps in the market that you can tap into.

4. Guest Interviews: Invite experts, professionals, and influencers from your niche to be guests on your podcast. They can provide

valuable insights, share their experiences, and offer unique perspectives. Guest interviews not only add credibility to your show but also attract a wider audience.

5. Storytelling: Incorporate storytelling techniques into your podcast episodes. Narrate personal anecdotes, success stories, or even fictional tales that connect with your audience emotionally. Storytelling makes your content relatable, engaging, and memorable.

6. Listener Feedback: Actively seek feedback from your listeners. Encourage them to leave comments, reviews, and suggestions. Analyze their feedback to understand what topics they find most interesting and valuable. This will help you tailor your content to meet their expectations.

7. Collaborations: Collaborate with other podcasters, content creators, or brands in your niche. This can be in the form of cross-promotion, joint episodes, or hosting events together. Collaborations expose your podcast to a wider audience and bring fresh perspectives to your content.

Remember, creating engaging content is an ongoing process. Continuously evaluate the performance of your episodes, experiment with different formats, and evolve your content strategy based on feedback and data. By consistently delivering valuable and captivating content, you will build a loyal following and establish your podcast as a go-to resource in your niche.

Developing a Content Schedule

In order to run a successful podcast, it is essential to have a well-thought-out content schedule. A content schedule helps you stay organized, ensures consistency, and keeps your audience engaged. In this subchapter, we will explore the key steps to developing a content schedule that caters to the interests of entrepreneurs, business professionals, music professionals, sports enthusiasts, sports professionals, musicians, film graduates, film professionals, and other niche audiences.

1. Identify Your Target Audience: Before starting your podcast, it is crucial to understand who your target audience is. Are you catering to aspiring entrepreneurs, music professionals, or sports enthusiasts? Knowing your audience will help you curate relevant content that resonates with them.

2. Research and Brainstorm Topics: Conduct thorough research and brainstorm a list of topics that align with your target audience's interests. For entrepreneurs, you might focus on start-up strategies, personal development, and self-improvement. For sports enthusiasts, consider discussing the latest sports news, athlete interviews, and analysis.

3. Create a Content Calendar: Once you have your list of topics, create a content calendar. This calendar should outline the specific topics you will cover in each episode and the release dates. Be realistic with your schedule and consider factors such as guest availability, research time, and editing requirements.

4. Consider Seasonal and Timely Content: To keep your podcast fresh and engaging, include seasonal and timely content. For example, during the holiday season, you might feature episodes on stress management or gift-giving tips. Stay up-to-date with industry trends and current events to provide valuable insights to your audience.

5. Balance and Variety: A well-rounded podcast appeals to a wider range of listeners. Ensure you offer a balance of topics and incorporate variety into your content schedule. For example, if you primarily focus on personal development, consider adding episodes on health and wellness, technology and innovation, or even comedy and entertainment.

6. Plan for Guest Interviews and Collaborations: Guest interviews and collaborations can bring a fresh perspective to your podcast.

Identify potential guests or collaborators in your niche and plan episodes around their availability. Having a diverse range of voices and expertise will enhance the value of your podcast.

Remember, developing a content schedule is an ongoing process. Continuously evaluate your episodes' performance and collect feedback from your audience. Adapt your schedule accordingly to ensure you are consistently delivering high-quality content that resonates with your target audience.

Whether you are starting a podcast in 2024, focusing on personal development, health and wellness, or catering to sports enthusiasts, a well-developed content schedule will be the backbone of your podcast's success. Take the time to plan, research, and curate engaging topics that will keep your audience coming back for more.

Scripting vs. Improvisation

When it comes to podcasting, one of the key decisions you'll need to make is whether to script your episodes or go with a more improvisational approach. Both methods have their pros and cons, and ultimately, the choice will depend on your personal style and the goals of your podcast.

Scripting your episodes can provide a sense of structure and control. It allows you to carefully craft your content, ensuring that every word is deliberate and impactful. This can be particularly beneficial for podcasts focused on personal development and self-improvement, as well as health and wellness podcasts. By scripting your episodes, you can deliver information in a clear and concise manner, making it easier for your audience to follow along and absorb the valuable insights you share.

Entrepreneurs and business professionals may also find scripting beneficial as it allows for a more polished and professional presentation. Technology and innovation podcasts can benefit from a scripted approach as it allows for a more focused and detailed discussion of complex topics.

On the other hand, improvisation can bring a sense of authenticity and spontaneity to your podcast. For comedy and entertainment podcasts, improvisation is often the preferred method as it allows hosts to react in real-time and create genuine moments of laughter and entertainment. Musicians and sports enthusiasts may also find that an improvisational approach allows for more engaging and dynamic conversations.

Film graduates and professionals may appreciate the flexibility of improvisation, as it allows for more natural and organic storytelling. This can be particularly beneficial for podcasts about travel and adventure, where hosts can share their experiences and emotions in a more authentic and unscripted manner.

Ultimately, the decision between scripting and improvisation will depend on your personal style, the goals of your podcast, and the preferences of your target audience. Some podcasters may even choose to combine both methods, using a script as a foundation but allowing room for improvisation and spontaneity.

No matter which approach you choose, remember that the most important thing is to stay true to your voice and deliver content that resonates with your audience. Whether scripted or improvised, a well-executed podcast will captivate and inspire your listeners, setting you up for success in the exciting world of podcasting.

Chapter 4: Recording and Editing

Recording Techniques and Best Practices

In the fast-paced world of podcasting, having high-quality audio is crucial to attract and retain listeners. Whether you are a seasoned podcaster or just starting out, understanding recording techniques and implementing best practices can significantly enhance the overall production value of your podcast. This subchapter will provide valuable insights and practical tips to help you achieve professional-grade audio recordings.

1. Choose the right microphone: Selecting the right microphone is essential for capturing clear and crisp audio. Consider factors such as budget, recording environment, and intended use when making your choice. Condenser microphones are popular for their sensitivity and accuracy, while dynamic microphones are more durable and suitable for recording in less controlled environments.

2. Invest in acoustic treatment: Soundproofing and acoustic treatment can greatly improve the audio quality by reducing echo and background noise. Consider using soundproofing foam panels, bass traps, and diffusers to create a more controlled recording environment.

3. Find the optimal recording space: Look for a quiet room with minimal outside noise and distractions. Avoid rooms with hard surfaces that can cause reflections and echo. Experiment with different locations until you find the best spot for recording.

4. Use a pop filter: A pop filter is a screen placed in front of the microphone to reduce plosive sounds caused by strong bursts of air, such as "p" and "b" sounds. This simple tool can significantly improve the clarity of your recordings.

5. Mind your microphone technique: Maintain a consistent distance from the microphone to achieve consistent audio levels. Avoid moving around or touching the microphone during recording to minimize unwanted noise.

6. Monitor and adjust audio levels: Use headphones to monitor your audio while recording. Keep an eye on the levels and adjust them accordingly to prevent clipping or distortion. Aim for a balanced mix between the speaker's voice and any background music or sound effects.

7. Consider remote recording options: In the era of remote work and virtual meetings, remote recording options have become increasingly popular. Explore platforms and tools that allow for high-quality remote interviews or collaborations.

By implementing these recording techniques and best practices, you can elevate your podcasting game and provide an enjoyable listening experience for your audience. Remember, great content deserves great audio quality. Take the time to invest in your podcast's production value, and watch it flourish in the competitive podcasting landscape.

This subchapter is particularly relevant for entrepreneurs, business professionals, music professionals, sports enthusiasts, sports professionals, musicians, film graduates, film professionals, and individuals interested in starting a podcast in 2024. Additionally, it caters to niche interests such as podcasts for aspiring entrepreneurs, personal development and self-improvement, health and wellness, technology and innovation, comedy and entertainment, travel and adventure, and sports enthusiasts.

Editing Your Podcast Episodes

As a podcaster, the content you create is crucial to the success of your show. However, it's equally important to ensure that the quality of your episodes is top-notch. This is where the editing process comes into play. Editing your podcast episodes is an essential step that can greatly enhance the overall listening experience for your audience. In this subchapter, we will explore the various aspects of editing and provide you with practical tips and techniques to make your podcast sound professional and engaging.

First and foremost, it's crucial to invest in a good editing software. There are plenty of options available, both free and paid, that offer a wide range of features to help you enhance your audio. Experiment with different software to find the one that suits your needs and budget.

Once you have your software in place, it's time to dive into the editing process. Start by listening to your raw recording and taking note of any mistakes, background noise, or long pauses. Trim these sections to create a smooth and seamless flow. Remember, your audience's attention span is limited, so keeping your episodes concise and engaging is key.

Next, pay attention to the overall audio quality. Adjust the volume levels to ensure a consistent sound throughout the episode. Use equalization to balance the frequencies and remove any unwanted noise or distortion. Adding music or sound effects can also enhance the listening experience, but be mindful not to overpower the main content.

In addition to technical aspects, consider the pacing and structure of your episodes. Edit out any unnecessary tangents or long-winded explanations to keep your content focused and concise. Use transitions, such as fade-ins and fade-outs, to create a professional and polished feel.

Lastly, always listen to the final edited version before publishing. Check for any remaining errors or glitches and make any necessary adjustments. It's also a good idea to get feedback from trusted friends or colleagues in your industry. Their fresh perspective can help you identify areas for improvement and ensure that your podcast meets the expectations of your target audience.

In conclusion, editing your podcast episodes is a crucial step in creating a professional and engaging listening experience. By investing in good editing software, being attentive to audio quality, pacing, and structure, and seeking feedback from others, you can elevate your podcast to new heights. So, grab your headphones and get ready to transform your raw recordings into captivating episodes that will keep your audience coming back for more.

Adding Intro and Outro Music

One of the key elements that can make your podcast stand out and create a memorable experience for your listeners is the use of intro and outro music. This chapter will guide you on how to select and incorporate the perfect music for your podcast.

For entrepreneurs and business professionals, intro and outro music can set the tone for your show and enhance your brand image. It should reflect your professionalism and the essence of your business. Consider using instrumental tracks that convey a sense of motivation and inspiration.

Music professionals, musicians, and film graduates can leverage their expertise in selecting the right intro and outro music for their podcasts. Use your creative flair to choose tracks that align with the genre or theme of your podcast. This will help create a cohesive and immersive experience for your audience.

Sports enthusiasts and professionals can opt for energetic and upbeat music that captures the excitement and passion of the sporting world. Consider using tracks with a strong rhythm or anthemic melodies to get your listeners pumped up.

For those focused on personal development and self-improvement, intro and outro music should be calming and soothing. Instrumental tracks with gentle melodies or ambient sounds can help create a relaxed and introspective atmosphere for your listeners.

Health and wellness podcasts can benefit from using calming and healing music. Look for tracks with nature sounds, soft piano, or gentle strings to create a peaceful and rejuvenating ambiance.

In the realm of technology and innovation podcasts, consider using futuristic and electronic music to match the theme. Tracks with synthesizers, bleeps, and beats can create an atmosphere of innovation and curiosity.

Comedy and entertainment podcasts can play with a wide range of music styles to match the tone of their show. From quirky and playful tunes to catchy jingles, the possibilities are endless.

Podcasts about travel and adventure can transport listeners to different places through the use of captivating intro and outro music. Consider using tracks with ethnic instruments, vibrant rhythms, and atmospheric sounds to evoke a sense of wanderlust.

Lastly, podcasts for sports enthusiasts can use intro and outro music that captures the intensity and excitement of the game. Look for tracks with powerful beats, electric guitar riffs, or energetic orchestral arrangements to create an adrenaline-pumping experience. Remember to keep your intro and outro music short and sweet, ideally between 10 to 30 seconds. This ensures that it doesn't overshadow the main content of your podcast. Be mindful of copyright laws and consider using royalty-free music or purchasing licenses for copyrighted tracks.

By carefully selecting and incorporating the right intro and outro music into your podcast, you can create a captivating and immersive experience for your audience. It will enhance your brand image, set the tone, and leave a lasting impression on your listeners. So, get creative and let the music elevate your podcast to new heights.

Enhancing Audio Quality

In the fast-paced world of podcasting, audio quality is a crucial factor that can make or break the success of your show. Whether you are a seasoned podcaster or just starting out, ensuring top-notch audio quality is essential to captivate your audience and keep them coming back for more. In this subchapter, we will explore various techniques and tools to enhance the audio quality of your podcast, ensuring a professional and engaging listening experience for your audience.

One of the first steps to improving your audio quality is investing in a high-quality microphone. A good microphone can make a world of difference in terms of clarity and richness of the sound. There are plenty of options available in the market, ranging from entry-level microphones for beginners to professional-grade ones for more advanced users. Take the time to research and choose a microphone that suits your needs and budget.

Another important aspect to consider is the environment in which you record your podcast. Background noise and echoes can significantly degrade the audio quality. To minimize these issues, it is advisable to record in a quiet and acoustically treated room. You can use soundproofing materials or blankets to absorb unwanted noise and create a more controlled recording environment.

Post-production editing plays a crucial role in enhancing the audio quality of your podcast. Investing in a good audio editing software can help you eliminate background noise, adjust levels, and make your voice sound more polished. Additionally, adding music and sound effects can add depth and professionalism to your podcast. For those looking for a more advanced approach, consider using a mixer or audio interface. These tools allow you to have more control over the audio input and output, resulting in a cleaner and more professional sound. They also give you the flexibility to connect multiple microphones and other audio devices, making them ideal for interviews or panel discussions.

Lastly, don't forget to regularly monitor and evaluate the audio quality of your podcast. Take the time to listen to your episodes critically and identify areas for improvement. Solicit feedback from your audience and make necessary adjustments to ensure a consistently high-quality listening experience.

In conclusion, audio quality is a vital element of podcasting that should not be overlooked. By investing in the right equipment, creating a suitable recording environment, and utilizing post-production techniques, you can enhance the audio quality of your podcast and provide your audience with an immersive and enjoyable listening experience. So, whether you are starting a podcast in 2024, focusing on personal development or self-improvement, technology and innovation, or any other niche, prioritize audio quality to stand out from the crowd and make your podcast a success.

Chapter 5: Launching Your Podcast

Choosing a Podcast Hosting Platform

In the world of podcasting, one of the most crucial decisions you'll make is selecting the right hosting platform. A podcast hosting platform is where you'll upload and store your podcast episodes, ensuring they are available to your listeners across various podcast directories and platforms. With the plethora of options available, it's important to consider several factors before making your choice. First and foremost, you need to ensure that your hosting platform is reliable and has a track record of minimal downtime. After all, the last thing you want is for your listeners to encounter difficulties accessing your episodes. Look for a platform that guarantees high uptime and provides robust technical support to resolve any issues promptly.

Next, consider the scalability of the hosting platform. As your podcast grows, you'll want a platform that can accommodate increasing storage needs and handle a larger number of listeners without compromising on speed or quality. Make sure the platform you choose can handle your podcast's growth trajectory, allowing you to focus on creating great content instead of worrying about technical limitations.

Another crucial factor is the platform's distribution capabilities. A good hosting platform will automatically distribute your podcast to major podcast directories like Apple Podcasts, Spotify, Google Podcasts, and more. This ensures that your podcast reaches a wider audience and maximizes your chances of gaining new listeners. Look for a platform that offers seamless integration with popular directories and platforms, making it easier for you to reach your target audience.

Furthermore, consider the platform's analytics and monetization features. Analytics allow you to track your podcast's performance, providing insights into listener demographics, engagement, and popular episodes. Monetization features, such as integrated advertising or sponsorship opportunities, can help you generate revenue from your podcast. Choose a hosting platform that offers robust analytics and monetization options to help you make informed decisions and potentially monetize your podcast.

Lastly, consider the user experience and interface of the hosting platform. A user-friendly platform will make it easier for you to upload, manage, and publish your episodes. Look for features like episode scheduling, easy editing, and customizable podcast pages that enhance your overall podcasting experience.

In conclusion, selecting the right podcast hosting platform is pivotal to the success of your podcast. Consider factors like reliability, scalability, distribution capabilities, analytics, monetization features, and user experience. By taking the time to evaluate these factors, you'll be better equipped to choose a hosting platform that aligns with your podcasting goals and ensures a seamless experience for your audience.

This subchapter is particularly relevant to entrepreneurs, business professionals, music professionals, sports enthusiasts, sports professionals, musicians, film graduates, film professionals, and those interested in starting a podcast in 2024, podcasts focused on personal development and self-improvement, health and wellness podcasts, technology and innovation podcasts, comedy and entertainment podcasts, podcasts about travel and adventure, and podcasts for sports enthusiasts.

Submitting to Podcast Directories

Once you have created and polished your podcast episodes, it's time to share your content with the world. One of the most effective ways to do this is by submitting your podcast to various podcast directories. These directories act as platforms that host and distribute podcasts, making it easier for your target audience to discover and listen to your show. In this subchapter, we will explore the importance of submitting to podcast directories and provide a step-by-step guide to help you navigate this process successfully. Submitting your podcast to directories is crucial because it significantly increases your show's visibility and reach. By listing your podcast on popular directories like Apple Podcasts, Spotify, Google Podcasts, and Stitcher, you can tap into their vast user base and attract a larger audience. This exposure can lead to more subscribers, downloads, and ultimately, success for your podcast. To begin, you need to create an account on each directory you wish to submit your podcast to. Many directories provide a straightforward sign-up process that requires basic information about your show, such as the podcast's title, description, artwork, and RSS feed. It is essential to optimize these elements to make your podcast stand out and entice potential listeners to click and listen. Once your podcast is approved and listed on the directories, you must regularly update your content to keep your show fresh and engaging. Adding new episodes, improving the show's description, and updating your podcast artwork are all ways to maintain your podcast's attractiveness and relevance.

Additionally, actively promoting your podcast on social media platforms, your website, and other relevant channels will help increase your show's visibility and attract more listeners. Engaging with your audience through comments, reviews, and feedback also fosters a sense of community around your podcast and encourages listeners to share your content with others.

Remember, submitting to podcast directories is just the first step in your podcasting journey. To succeed and stand out in today's competitive landscape, you must consistently produce high-quality content, engage with your audience, and adapt to changing trends and listener preferences.

Whether you are an aspiring entrepreneur, a business professional, a sports enthusiast, or a film graduate, podcasting presents a unique opportunity to share your knowledge, experiences, and passion with the world. By submitting your podcast to directories, you can reach a wider audience and establish yourself as a reputable voice in your niche. So, take the plunge, submit your podcast to directories, and let your voice be heard in the thriving podcasting community.

Creating Eye-Catching Cover Art

In today's digital age, where attention spans are shorter than ever, having eye-catching cover art for your podcast is crucial. Your cover art is the first thing potential listeners will see, and it needs to grab their attention and make them want to click play. In this subchapter, we will discuss the importance of creating visually appealing cover art and provide practical tips to help you design a cover that stands out.

Entrepreneurs, business professionals, music professionals, sports enthusiasts, sports professionals, musicians, film graduates, film professionals, and anyone looking to start a podcast in 2024 will benefit from this valuable advice. Additionally, individuals interested in podcasts focused on personal development and self-improvement, health and wellness, technology and innovation, comedy and entertainment, or travel and adventure will find these tips useful.

When it comes to designing cover art, simplicity is key. You want your artwork to be visually striking but not overwhelming. Choose a clean and minimalist design that clearly represents the theme or topic of your podcast. Use bold colors and fonts that are easy to read, even when the image is small.

Consider incorporating relevant imagery that instantly communicates your podcast's content. For example, if you're hosting a health and wellness podcast, include icons related to fitness or healthy eating. If your podcast focuses on travel and adventure, use images that evoke a sense of wanderlust. The goal is to create an emotional connection with your potential audience right from the start.

Another important factor to keep in mind is scalability. Your cover art should look great on various platforms, from podcast directories to social media profiles. Test your design on different devices to ensure it's legible and visually appealing, regardless of the screen size.

Lastly, don't be afraid to get creative and experiment with different concepts. Look for inspiration in other successful podcasts but strive to make your cover art unique and memorable. Consider hiring a professional graphic designer if you lack design skills or need assistance in bringing your vision to life.

Remember, your podcast cover art is your visual calling card. It's what will grab the attention of potential listeners and entice them to give your podcast a chance. By following these tips and putting effort into creating eye-catching cover art, you'll be one step closer to success in the competitive world of podcasting.

Promoting Your Podcast on Social Media

In today's digital age, social media has become an indispensable tool for promoting any kind of content, and podcasts are no exception. With millions of users worldwide, platforms like Facebook, Twitter, Instagram, and LinkedIn offer tremendous opportunities to reach and engage with your target audience. In this subchapter, we will explore effective strategies for promoting your podcast on social media to maximize its reach and impact.

1. Create Engaging Visual Content: When promoting your podcast on social media, it's crucial to capture your audience's attention with eye-catching visuals. Design compelling graphics, such as custom episode artwork, teaser images, and behind-the-scenes photos, to accompany your social media posts. These visuals will make your content more shareable and increase its visibility.

2. Leverage Influencer Partnerships: Collaborating with influencers in your niche can significantly boost your podcast's visibility and credibility. Identify influencers or industry experts who align with your podcast's topic and reach out to them for potential partnerships. They can help spread the word about your podcast to their followers and attract new listeners.

3. Encourage User-generated Content: Engaging with your audience is crucial for building a loyal community around your podcast. Encourage your listeners to share their thoughts, reviews, and recommendations about your episodes on social media. User-generated content not only helps you understand your audience better but also serves as powerful social proof to attract new listeners.

4. Run Contests and Giveaways: People love freebies, and running contests or giveaways on social media is an excellent way to

generate buzz around your podcast. Create enticing prizes related to your podcast's niche and ask your audience to engage with your content by liking, sharing, or commenting on your posts. This will not only increase your social media reach but also incentivize your existing audience to become brand ambassadors.

5. Cross-promote with Other Podcasters: Collaboration is key in the podcasting community. Reach out to other podcasters in your niche and propose cross-promotion opportunities. This can involve guest appearances on each other's shows, shout-outs on social media, or simply recommending each other's podcasts to your respective audiences. By tapping into each other's fan base, you can significantly expand your reach.

6. Engage in Active Community Management: Building an engaged community around your podcast is vital for long-term success. Regularly monitor and respond to comments, direct messages, and mentions on social media. Engaging with your audience not only strengthens the bond but also helps you understand their preferences and tailor your content accordingly.

By implementing these strategies, you can effectively promote your podcast on social media and attract a wider audience. Remember, consistency and engagement are key to building a thriving podcast community, so make sure to stay active and responsive across your social media platforms.

Chapter 6: Growing Your Audience

Strategies for Increasing Podcast Downloads

If you have recently started your own podcast or are planning to launch one in 2024, you may be wondering how to increase your podcast downloads and reach a wider audience. In this subchapter, we will explore effective strategies that will help you grow your podcast and attract more listeners.

1. Optimize your podcast for search engines: Just like websites, podcasts can also be optimized for search engines. Conduct keyword research relevant to your podcast's niche and incorporate those keywords in your episode titles, descriptions, and show notes. This will make it easier for potential listeners to find your podcast when searching for related topics.

2. Promote your podcast on social media: Leverage the power of social media to expand your podcast's reach. Create dedicated profiles on platforms like Facebook, Instagram, Twitter, and LinkedIn, and regularly share engaging content related to your podcast. Encourage your existing listeners to share your episodes with their network to increase visibility.

3. Collaborate with influencers and industry experts: Reach out to influencers and industry experts within your niche and invite them to be guests on your podcast. Their existing audience will be more likely to listen to your episodes, increasing your podcast's visibility and credibility.

4. Cross-promote with other podcasts: Identify other podcasts that share a similar target audience and collaborate with their hosts to cross-promote each other's shows. This can be done through guest appearances, shout-outs, or even joint episodes. By tapping into their established listener base, you can gain exposure to a wider audience.

5. Provide valuable and unique content: The key to attracting and retaining listeners is to consistently provide valuable and unique content. Research your target audience's interests and pain points and tailor your episodes to address those needs. Engage with your audience through email newsletters, polls, and Q&A sessions to ensure you are delivering content they find valuable.

6. Encourage listener engagement and reviews: Actively encourage your listeners to engage with your podcast by leaving reviews, ratings, and comments. Positive reviews and ratings not only boost your podcast's credibility but also improve its visibility in podcast directories.

7. Utilize email marketing: Build an email list of your podcast listeners and regularly communicate with them through newsletters. Share updates, upcoming episode teasers, and exclusive content to keep your audience engaged and excited about your podcast.

Remember, increasing podcast downloads takes time and effort. Consistency, quality content, and effective promotion strategies will help you build a loyal listener base and grow your podcast steadily.

Engaging with Your Audience

One of the most crucial aspects of podcasting is building a strong connection with your audience. Whether you are an entrepreneur, business professional, music enthusiast, sports professional, or anyone else in the niches of podcasting, engaging with your audience is key to creating a successful podcast.

When starting your podcast in 2024, it's important to remember that your audience is your biggest asset. They are the ones who will listen, support, and promote your podcast. Therefore, it is essential to establish a strong connection with them right from the beginning.

First and foremost, understand your target audience. Entrepreneurs and business professionals might be looking for podcasts focused on personal development and self-improvement. Music professionals may be interested in podcasts that discuss the latest trends in the industry. Sports enthusiasts would be eager to listen to podcasts that cover their favorite sports and provide expert analysis. Film graduates and professionals might enjoy podcasts that delve into the world of filmmaking and offer valuable insights.

To engage with your audience effectively, it's crucial to create content that resonates with them. Tailor your podcast episodes to address their interests and needs. Incorporate interviews, discussions, and expert opinions to add value to your episodes. Encourage your listeners to provide feedback and suggestions, and be responsive to their comments. This will make them feel valued and will keep them coming back for more.

Utilize social media platforms to enhance engagement. Share behind-the-scenes content, teasers, and updates about upcoming episodes. Encourage your audience to interact with you on social media by asking questions and initiating discussions. This will not only boost engagement but also help you understand your audience better.

Consider organizing live events or meetups where you can interact with your audience face-to-face. This personal touch can create a deep connection and foster a loyal fan base.

Lastly, never underestimate the power of storytelling. Humans are wired to connect with stories. Incorporate compelling narratives into your podcast episodes to captivate your audience's attention and keep them engaged throughout.

In conclusion, engaging with your audience is the key to a successful podcast. By understanding your target audience, creating valuable content, utilizing social media, and incorporating storytelling, you can build a strong connection with your listeners. Remember, your audience is your biggest asset, so make them feel heard, valued, and excited about what you have to offer.

Collaborating with Other Podcasters

Podcasting has exploded in popularity in recent years, and it's no wonder why. It provides a unique platform for individuals to share their ideas, stories, and expertise with a global audience. However, with so many podcasts vying for attention, it can be challenging to stand out from the crowd. That's where collaborating with other podcasters can make a significant difference.

Collaboration is key in any industry, and podcasting is no exception. By joining forces with other podcasters, you can tap into their existing audience and gain exposure to a whole new group of listeners. This is especially beneficial for entrepreneurs and business professionals who are looking to expand their reach and attract new clients or customers.

For music professionals, collaborating with other podcasters can be an excellent way to promote their music and gain new fans. By featuring your music on a podcast, you can reach a broader audience and increase your chances of getting discovered.

Sports enthusiasts and professionals can also benefit from collaborating with other podcasters in the same niche. By teaming up with other sports-focused podcasts, you can provide a more comprehensive and engaging listening experience for your audience. This can lead to increased listenership and opportunities for sponsorship and partnerships.

Similarly, film graduates and professionals can collaborate with other podcasters in the film industry. By discussing the latest movies, sharing behind-the-scenes stories, and interviewing industry experts, you can attract film enthusiasts and build a loyal following.

Podcasts focused on personal development and self-improvement can also benefit from collaboration. By featuring guest experts and hosting joint episodes with other podcasters in the same niche, you can provide diverse perspectives and valuable insights to your audience.

Collaboration is not limited to specific niches. Health and wellness podcasts, technology and innovation podcasts, comedy and entertainment podcasts, and podcasts about travel and adventure can all find value in collaborating with other podcasters. By pooling resources, sharing audiences, and cross-promoting each other's content, you can create a win-win situation for everyone involved.

In conclusion, collaborating with other podcasters is a powerful strategy that can help you grow your podcast and reach a wider audience. Whether you're an entrepreneur, business professional, music enthusiast, sports enthusiast, filmmaker, or belong to any other niche, there are endless opportunities for collaboration in the podcasting world. So, reach out to other podcasters, explore partnership opportunities, and watch your podcast soar to new heights in 2024 and beyond.

Leveraging Guest Interviews

One of the most powerful tools in the world of podcasting is the ability to bring on guest interviews. As a podcaster, you have the opportunity to connect with experts, thought leaders, and influencers in your niche, and share their knowledge and insights with your audience. Leveraging guest interviews can take your podcast to new heights, attracting a wider audience and establishing yourself as a trusted authority in your field. In this subchapter, we will explore the benefits of guest interviews and provide you with strategies to make the most out of these valuable opportunities.

For entrepreneurs and business professionals, guest interviews can provide valuable insights and inspiration. By inviting successful entrepreneurs and industry leaders to share their stories and expertise, you can offer your audience practical tips, advice, and strategies for starting and growing their own businesses. Moreover, music professionals, sports enthusiasts, and film graduates can tap into the knowledge and experiences of experts in their respective fields, gaining valuable insights into the industry and potentially opening new doors for their careers.

If your podcast is focused on personal development and self-improvement, guest interviews can be a game-changer. By bringing on experts in psychology, mindfulness, and motivation, you can provide your listeners with the tools and techniques they need to enhance their personal and professional lives. Health and wellness podcasts can leverage guest interviews to feature doctors, nutritionists, and fitness experts who can share their expertise and help your audience make positive changes in their lives.

Technology and innovation podcasts can benefit from guest interviews with tech industry leaders, entrepreneurs, and inventors. By discussing the latest trends, breakthroughs, and developments, you can keep your audience informed and engaged. On the other hand, comedy and entertainment podcasts can bring on comedians, actors, and entertainers to share their funny anecdotes and experiences, providing a dose of laughter and entertainment to your listeners.

For the adventurous souls and sports enthusiasts, guest interviews with travel experts, explorers, and athletes can offer exciting stories and insights into the world of travel and adventure. Whether it's tips for planning the perfect trip or tales of thrilling expeditions, these interviews can inspire your audience to embark on their own adventures.

In conclusion, leveraging guest interviews is a powerful tool in the world of podcasting. It allows you to tap into the knowledge and experiences of experts, thought leaders, and influencers in your niche, providing valuable content to your audience. By incorporating guest interviews into your podcast, you can attract a wider audience, establish yourself as an authority, and take your podcast to new heights.

Chapter 7: Monetizing Your Podcast

Sponsorships and Advertisements

In the world of podcasting, sponsorships and advertisements play a crucial role in the success and monetization of your show. Whether you are an aspiring entrepreneur, a business professional, a music enthusiast, or a sports professional, understanding how to effectively incorporate sponsorships and advertisements into your podcast can open up new opportunities and revenue streams.

Start a podcast in 2024 and build a loyal audience around your niche. As you gain traction and attract listeners, brands and companies will start to take notice. Sponsorships can be a win-win situation, where you promote their products or services in exchange for financial support or other benefits. However, it is essential to ensure that the sponsorship aligns with your podcast's theme and values, as authenticity is key to maintaining your audience's trust.

Podcasts focused on personal development and self-improvement have a vast potential for sponsorships. Health and wellness brands, lifestyle products, and even coaching services could be interested in reaching your audience. By carefully selecting sponsors that genuinely provide value to your listeners, you can create a mutually beneficial relationship that enhances your podcast's credibility and offers valuable content to your audience.

Technology and innovation podcasts are also hotspots for sponsorships. Companies in the tech industry are constantly looking for ways to promote their latest gadgets, software, or services. As a podcast host in this niche, you can leverage your expertise to showcase these products or services to your listeners, while generating income from these sponsorships.

Comedy and entertainment podcasts can also attract sponsorships from various brands. Companies that cater to the entertainment industry, such as streaming platforms, event organizers, or even comedy clubs, may be interested in partnering with you to reach your audience. These partnerships can not only generate revenue but also provide exciting opportunities for collaborations and guest appearances.

If you have a podcast about travel and adventure, sponsorships from travel agencies, hotels, or outdoor gear brands can be a perfect fit.

Your podcast can serve as a platform to share travel stories, tips, and recommendations, making it an attractive advertising opportunity for companies in the travel industry.

Sports enthusiasts will find sponsorships from sports-related brands particularly relevant. Sports apparel, equipment manufacturers, or even sports media outlets may want to collaborate with you to promote their products or events to your audience. By incorporating these sponsorships into your podcast, you can enhance the sports experience for your listeners while generating income.

In conclusion, sponsorships and advertisements can be a vital part of your podcast's success and monetization. As an entrepreneur, business professional, music enthusiast, or sports professional, understanding how to effectively incorporate sponsorships into your podcast can open up new opportunities and revenue streams. By selecting sponsors that align with your podcast's theme and values, you can create authentic partnerships that benefit both your audience and your podcast's growth. So, start exploring the possibilities of sponsorships and advertisements in your podcasting journey and unlock the full potential of your show.

Creating Merchandise and Patreon Support

As a podcast host, there are several ways to monetize your show and turn your passion into a profitable venture. In this subchapter, we will explore two popular methods: creating merchandise and utilizing Patreon for support. Whether you're a business professional, musician, or sports enthusiast, these strategies can help you generate additional income and grow your podcasting empire.

Merchandise is a fantastic way to engage with your audience and provide them with tangible products that showcase their love for your podcast. Entrepreneurs and business professionals can create branded merchandise such as t-shirts, mugs, or even custom-made notebooks featuring their podcast's logo. Music professionals can offer exclusive merchandise like signed albums or limited edition merchandise bundles. Sports enthusiasts can develop merchandise that showcases their favorite teams or athletes, from jerseys to caps and beyond. Film graduates and professionals can create merchandise inspired by their favorite movies or TV shows, allowing their audience to wear their fandom proudly.

Another avenue to explore is Patreon, a platform that enables creators to receive ongoing financial support from their dedicated listeners. By offering bonus content, early access to episodes, or even personalized shoutouts, Patreon allows entrepreneurs, musicians, and sports professionals to cultivate a loyal community of supporters. Film graduates and professionals can provide behind-the-scenes footage, exclusive interviews, or even private film screenings to their Patreon subscribers. This platform is also ideal for podcasters focused on personal development, health and wellness, technology and innovation, comedy and entertainment, and even travel and adventure.

For sports enthusiasts, Patreon can provide a space to offer premium sports-related content, such as in-depth analysis, interviews with athletes or coaches, and insider information. Similarly, music professionals can grant their Patreon supporters access to exclusive music releases, live performances, or even virtual meet-and-greets.

By combining merchandise sales and Patreon support, podcasters can create a sustainable income stream while strengthening the bond with their audience. This dual strategy allows entrepreneurs, business professionals, music professionals, sports enthusiasts, film graduates, and professionals to transform their podcasting aspirations into a profitable and fulfilling endeavor.

Remember, as you venture into creating merchandise and utilizing Patreon, always prioritize the needs and desires of your audience. Provide them with high-quality products and exclusive content that aligns with their interests, and your podcast will continue to grow as a thriving and profitable enterprise.

Crowdfunding and Donations

In today's digital age, crowdfunding has emerged as a powerful tool for entrepreneurs, musicians, filmmakers, and podcasters alike. Whether you're looking to start your own podcast, create content for aspiring entrepreneurs, or delve into the world of personal development and self-improvement, crowdfunding and donations can provide the necessary financial support to turn your dreams into reality.

For entrepreneurs and business professionals, crowdfunding offers an alternative to traditional financing methods. By harnessing the power of the crowd, you can tap into a vast network of potential investors who believe in your vision and are willing to contribute financially. Not only does this provide the necessary capital to launch your podcast, but it also serves as a validation of your idea, as people are putting their money where their faith lies.

Music professionals and sports enthusiasts can also benefit greatly from crowdfunding. With the rise of independent artists and athletes, crowdfunding platforms have become a popular avenue to fund albums, tours, and training expenses. By engaging with your fanbase and offering exclusive rewards, such as limited edition merchandise or personalized experiences, you can create a sense of community and loyalty that goes beyond financial support.

Filmmakers and film graduates, on the other hand, can utilize crowdfunding to bring their creative visions to life. With the increasing democratization of the film industry, crowdfunding has become an essential tool for independent filmmakers to secure funding for production, post-production, and distribution. By showcasing your unique story and leveraging social media, you can attract donors who are passionate about supporting emerging talent. Regardless of your niche, crowdfunding also provides an opportunity to give back to the community. Through donations, you can support charitable causes and make a positive impact on society. Health and wellness podcasts can raise funds for medical research, while technology and innovation podcasts can support initiatives that drive technological advancements. Comedy and entertainment podcasts can use crowdfunding to fund live shows or support organizations that promote mental health awareness. Similarly, podcasts about travel and adventure can rally donations to preserve natural wonders and promote sustainable tourism. Lastly, podcasts for sports enthusiasts can raise funds to provide equal opportunities for aspiring athletes or support initiatives that use sports as a vehicle for social change.

In conclusion, crowdfunding and donations have revolutionized the way individuals and businesses finance their creative endeavors. By leveraging the power of the crowd, you can turn your podcasting dreams into a reality, while also supporting causes and initiatives that align with your values. So, whether you're an entrepreneur, musician, filmmaker, or sports enthusiast, consider the vast potential of crowdfunding and donations in making a meaningful impact in your industry and beyond.

Selling Your Own Products or Services

Subchapter: Selling Your Own Products or Services
As a podcast host, you have a unique opportunity to monetize your show by selling your own products or services. This subchapter will

guide you through the process of leveraging your podcast platform to generate revenue and build a successful business.

For entrepreneurs and business professionals, podcasting can be an excellent way to showcase your expertise and attract potential clients. By offering valuable insights and practical advice on your show, you can establish yourself as a thought leader in your industry. This credibility can lead to new business opportunities, consulting gigs, or even speaking engagements.

Music professionals, sports enthusiasts, and film graduates can use podcasting as a medium to promote their work and connect with their audience. Whether you're a musician looking to sell your albums or a film graduate seeking collaborations, your podcast can serve as a powerful marketing tool. By sharing behind-the-scenes stories, exclusive content, and engaging interviews, you can build a dedicated fan base that is more likely to support your artistic endeavors.

Additionally, podcasting can be a great platform for selling products or services in various niches. For those interested in personal development and self-improvement, you can create online courses or coaching programs and promote them through your podcast. Health and wellness enthusiasts can sell fitness programs, nutritional supplements, or even branded merchandise to their dedicated listeners.

Technology and innovation podcasts can partner with relevant companies to promote their products or services, earning both a commission and building a reputation as a trusted source of information in the tech industry. Comedy and entertainment podcasts can sell merchandise, tickets to live shows, or even create a Patreon account to generate income from their loyal fan base.

Travel and adventure podcasts can partner with travel agencies, hotels, or travel gear companies to offer exclusive discounts to their listeners. Similarly, sports enthusiasts can collaborate with sports-related brands to promote their products or services, such as sports equipment, apparel, or event tickets.

In conclusion, podcasting offers a wide range of opportunities for monetization. By leveraging your expertise and building a loyal audience, you can create and sell your own products or services, generating income and building a successful business. Whether you're an entrepreneur, business professional, musician, film graduate, or sports enthusiast, podcasting can be the perfect platform to showcase your skills, connect with your target audience, and turn your passion into a profitable venture.

Chapter 8: Podcasting for Aspiring Entrepreneurs

Using Podcasting as a Marketing Tool

In today's digital age, podcasting has emerged as a powerful marketing tool that entrepreneurs, business professionals, and individuals from various industries can leverage to connect with their target audiences. Whether you are an aspiring entrepreneur, a music professional, a sports enthusiast, or a film graduate, podcasting offers an incredible opportunity to reach and engage with your audience in a unique and personal way.

Start a podcast in 2024 and unlock a world of possibilities for your brand or personal growth. Podcasting allows you to establish yourself as an industry expert, share your knowledge and insights, and build a loyal following. By creating valuable content that resonates with your target audience, you can position yourself as a thought leader and gain credibility in your niche.

For aspiring entrepreneurs, podcasting can be a game-changer. Start a podcast focused on personal development and self-improvement, providing valuable tips, strategies, and interviews with successful entrepreneurs. This not only helps you establish your expertise but also attracts like-minded individuals who are eager to learn and grow.

Health and wellness podcasts are also gaining popularity, as people are becoming more conscious of their well-being. If you are in the health industry, podcasting can be a great platform to share your knowledge, offer advice, and inspire others to lead a healthy lifestyle. Whether you specialize in nutrition, fitness, or mental health, a podcast allows you to connect with your audience on a deeper level and establish trust.

In the realm of technology and innovation, podcasting provides an avenue to discuss the latest trends, advancements, and industry insights. As a technology professional, you can share your expertise, interview industry experts, and provide valuable information to your listeners. This not only positions you as a thought leader but also attracts tech enthusiasts who are eager to stay updated with the latest developments.

However, podcasting is not limited to serious topics only. Comedy and entertainment podcasts have gained immense popularity, offering a much-needed escape from daily routines. If you have a knack for humor and entertainment, start a podcast that brings laughter and joy to your audience's lives. By creating engaging and entertaining content, you can attract a loyal fan base and even monetize your podcast through sponsorships and advertisements.

Furthermore, podcasts about travel and adventure are a hit among wanderlust enthusiasts. Share your travel experiences, provide destination guides, and inspire others to explore the world. Whether you are a seasoned traveler or an adventure enthusiast, podcasting allows you to share your passion and connect with fellow travel enthusiasts.

Lastly, for sports enthusiasts, podcasting provides a platform to discuss their favorite teams, players, and upcoming events. Engage with your audience by providing game analysis, interviews with sports professionals, and sharing your passion for the game. Sports podcasts are a fantastic way to create a community of like-minded individuals who share a common love for sports.

In conclusion, podcasting is a versatile and powerful marketing tool that can benefit entrepreneurs, business professionals, music professionals, sports enthusiasts, film graduates, and individuals from various niches. Whether you want to establish yourself as an industry expert, share your knowledge, entertain, or inspire, podcasting offers endless possibilities to connect with your audience and achieve your goals. Start your podcasting journey in 2024 and unlock the potential to make a lasting impact in your industry.

Building Your Personal Brand through Podcasting

In today's digital age, personal branding has become more important than ever. It is no longer enough to have a great product or service; you need to establish yourself as an authority in your field. One of the most effective ways to do this is through podcasting. In this subchapter, we will explore how you can build your personal brand through podcasting and leverage this powerful medium to reach a wide audience.

For entrepreneurs and business professionals, podcasting offers a unique opportunity to showcase your expertise and establish yourself as a thought leader in your industry. By hosting a podcast focused on your niche, you can share valuable insights, interview industry experts, and provide actionable advice to your listeners. This not only helps you build credibility but also attracts potential clients and customers to your business.

Similarly, for music professionals, podcasting can be a powerful tool to promote your work and connect with your audience. You can share your latest tracks, discuss the creative process, and even invite guest musicians to collaborate on your podcast. This helps you gain visibility in the industry and opens up new opportunities for collaborations and partnerships.

Sports enthusiasts and professionals can also benefit greatly from podcasting. By hosting a podcast dedicated to sports, you can share your passion, provide expert analysis, and engage with fellow enthusiasts. This helps you build a community of loyal followers and opens up opportunities for sponsorships and partnerships with sports brands.

For film graduates and professionals, podcasting offers a platform to discuss the latest trends, review films, and share behind-the-scenes stories. This helps you showcase your knowledge and insights, while also building a network within the film industry.

No matter your niche, podcasting can be a powerful tool for personal development and self-improvement. By hosting a podcast focused on personal growth, you can share tips, strategies, and inspiring stories to help your listeners improve their lives. This not only helps you build a loyal audience but also positions you as a trusted mentor and coach.

In conclusion, podcasting is an excellent way to build your personal brand and establish yourself as an authority in your field. Whether you are an entrepreneur, business professional, music professional, sports enthusiast, film graduate, or simply passionate about a particular topic, podcasting offers a unique opportunity to share your knowledge, connect with your audience, and build a strong personal brand. So, seize the opportunity and start podcasting in 2024!

Leveraging Podcasting for Networking Opportunities

In today's digital age, podcasting has emerged as a powerful tool for networking and establishing connections with like-minded individuals across various industries. Whether you are an entrepreneur, business professional, music enthusiast, sports professional, or anyone looking to expand your network, podcasting can be a game-changer for you. In this subchapter, we will explore the numerous networking opportunities that podcasting offers and how you can leverage them effectively.

For entrepreneurs and business professionals, starting a podcast in 2024 can be a smart move to showcase your expertise, share valuable insights, and attract potential clients or partners. By hosting interviews with industry leaders, sharing success stories, and discussing current trends, you can position yourself as a thought leader and gain credibility within your niche. Through podcasting, you can connect with influential individuals who can open doors to new business opportunities or collaborations.

If you are passionate about personal development and self-improvement, podcasting can provide an excellent platform to connect with experts and enthusiasts in this field. By hosting conversations on topics like mindfulness, motivation, productivity, and life hacks, you can engage with a community of individuals who share your interests. This can lead to meaningful connections, mentorship opportunities, and even collaborations on future projects. Health and wellness professionals can also leverage podcasting to reach a wider audience and establish themselves as authorities in their respective fields. By sharing expert advice, discussing the latest research, and interviewing industry experts, you can attract listeners who are seeking guidance on fitness, nutrition, mental health, and overall well-being. This can open doors to partnerships, speaking engagements, and even product endorsements.

For technology enthusiasts and innovators, podcasting offers a unique opportunity to showcase the latest advancements, discuss emerging trends, and connect with fellow tech enthusiasts. By hosting interviews with tech leaders, sharing insights on AI, blockchain, cybersecurity, or any other niche within the technology sector, you can build a network of like-minded individuals and potentially attract investors or collaborators.

If you have a knack for comedy and entertainment, podcasting can be a great way to connect with a broad audience and showcase your talent. By hosting a comedy podcast or an entertainment-focused show, you can build a loyal fan base, connect with fellow comedians or entertainers, and even attract potential gigs or collaborations.

Sports enthusiasts can also tap into the power of podcasting to share their passion and expertise with a dedicated audience. By hosting sports-focused podcasts, discussing game analysis, conducting interviews with athletes or sports professionals, you can connect with fellow fans and potentially attract sponsorship opportunities or media coverage.

Musicians and film professionals can use podcasting as a creative outlet to share their music, discuss the artistic process, and connect with fans and industry insiders. By hosting a podcast that explores the world of music or filmmaking, you can build a loyal following, attract potential collaborators, and even gain exposure for your work.

In conclusion, podcasting presents a plethora of networking opportunities for entrepreneurs, business professionals, music enthusiasts, sports professionals, and individuals from various niches. By leveraging the power of podcasting, you can connect with like-minded individuals, showcase your expertise, and open doors to new collaborations, partnerships, and career opportunities. So, don't miss out on this incredible tool to expand your network and take your career or passion to new heights.

Monetizing Your Entrepreneurial Knowledge

In today's digital age, where information is readily accessible, entrepreneurs have a unique opportunity to share their knowledge and expertise with a global audience through podcasting. This subchapter will delve into the various strategies for monetizing your entrepreneurial knowledge and turning your podcast into a profitable venture.

For entrepreneurs and business professionals, starting a podcast in 2024 is an excellent way to establish credibility and attract potential clients or customers. By sharing your insights, experiences, and tips on starting and growing a successful business, you can position yourself as an authority in your industry. This can lead to speaking engagements, consulting opportunities, or even partnerships with other businesses.

Podcasts focused on personal development and self-improvement are immensely popular, and there is a vast audience eager to learn from experts in this field. By providing valuable content and actionable advice on topics such as leadership, productivity, and goal-setting, you can build a loyal following and attract sponsors or advertisers who align with your podcast's theme.

Health and wellness podcasts have also gained significant traction in recent years, as people are increasingly prioritizing their physical and mental well-being. If you have expertise in nutrition, fitness, mindfulness, or any other health-related field, you can create a podcast that educates and inspires listeners to live a healthier lifestyle. This can open doors to collaborations with wellness brands, fitness influencers, or even the possibility of launching your own health-related products or services.

For technology enthusiasts and innovators, podcasting offers a platform to discuss the latest trends, innovations, and industry insights. By staying ahead of the curve and providing valuable information to your audience, you can attract sponsorships from tech companies, secure speaking engagements at tech conferences, or even launch your own tech-related products or services.

Comedy and entertainment podcasts are a great way to showcase your creativity and humor while building a loyal fan base. With the right mix of entertainment and engaging content, you can attract advertisers or even explore avenues such as live shows, merchandise, or collaborations with other comedians or entertainers.

For sports enthusiasts, a podcast dedicated to their favorite sport or team can be a goldmine. By analyzing games, interviewing athletes and coaches, and providing expert insights, you can attract sponsors from sports brands, secure partnerships with sports media outlets, or even explore opportunities to cover live sporting events.

Lastly, podcasts about travel and adventure can transport listeners to different parts of the world, offering valuable insights, tips, and stories. By partnering with travel agencies, hotels, or tourism boards, you can monetize your podcast through sponsored content, affiliate marketing, or even organizing group trips or tours.

In conclusion, podcasting offers entrepreneurs, business professionals, and enthusiasts from various niches the opportunity to monetize their knowledge and expertise. By consistently delivering valuable content, building a loyal audience, and exploring partnerships and sponsorships, you can turn your podcast into a thriving business venture. So, don't wait any longer – start podcasting and unlock the potential to monetize your entrepreneurial knowledge in 2024 and beyond.

Chapter 9: Podcasts for Personal Development and Self-Improvement

Exploring Motivational and Inspirational Podcasts

In today's fast-paced world, where the daily grind can often leave us feeling uninspired and unmotivated, podcasts have emerged as a powerful tool for personal development and self-improvement. Whether you're an entrepreneur, business professional, music enthusiast, or sports professional, there is a vast array of motivational and inspirational podcasts that can provide you with the boost of motivation and guidance you need to achieve your goals. For aspiring entrepreneurs, podcasts offer valuable insights and advice from successful business owners and industry experts. These podcasts delve into topics such as starting a business, marketing strategies, and overcoming challenges. By listening to these podcasts, you can gain valuable knowledge and inspiration to kickstart your entrepreneurial journey in 2024.

If personal development and self-improvement are your primary focus, there are numerous podcasts that offer guidance on topics like mindset, goal-setting, time management, and building positive habits. These podcasts are designed to help you unleash your full potential and achieve personal and professional success.

For health and wellness enthusiasts, podcasts provide a wealth of information on nutrition, fitness, mental health, and overall well-being. These podcasts feature experts in their respective fields who provide practical tips and advice to help you live a healthier and more fulfilling life.

In the rapidly evolving world of technology and innovation, staying updated is crucial. Technology and innovation podcasts offer insights into the latest trends, advancements, and disruptive technologies that are reshaping industries. By tuning in to these podcasts, you can stay ahead of the curve and gain a competitive edge in your field.

For those in need of a good laugh or some entertainment, comedy and entertainment podcasts are perfect. These podcasts feature comedians, storytellers, and entertainers who will keep you entertained and uplifted throughout your day.

If you have a passion for travel and adventure, there are podcasts that cater to your wanderlust. These podcasts take you on virtual journeys, sharing travel stories, tips, and destination recommendations. Whether you're planning your next trip or simply seeking inspiration, these podcasts will transport you to new and exciting places.

Lastly, for sports enthusiasts, there are podcasts that cover a wide range of sports, providing analysis, interviews, and behind-the-scenes stories. These podcasts allow you to stay connected to your favorite sports and athletes while gaining valuable insights and perspectives.

In conclusion, podcasts have become an essential resource for entrepreneurs, business professionals, music enthusiasts, sports professionals, and individuals from various niches. By exploring motivational and inspirational podcasts, you can find the guidance, motivation, and inspiration you need to excel in your chosen field and lead a more fulfilling life. So, grab your headphones, tune in, and let the power of podcasts propel you towards success in 2024 and beyond.

Delving into Mental Health and Well-being Podcasts

In recent years, the popularity of podcasts has skyrocketed, and for good reason. Podcasts offer a unique and convenient way to consume information and entertainment on the go. Whether you're commuting to work, hitting the gym, or simply relaxing at home, podcasts provide an immersive experience that keeps you engaged and informed. One genre that has gained significant traction is mental health and well-being podcasts.

Addressing the growing need for mental health awareness and self-improvement, these podcasts offer valuable insights, tips, and strategies to help individuals achieve optimal mental well-being. Entrepreneurs, business professionals, music professionals, sports enthusiasts, musicians, film graduates, and professionals from various fields can all benefit from delving into mental health and well-being podcasts.

For entrepreneurs and business professionals, mental health and well-being podcasts can provide valuable guidance on stress management, work-life balance, and building resilience. These podcasts often feature interviews with successful entrepreneurs who share their personal stories and offer practical advice on maintaining mental well-being while navigating the challenges of running a business.

For music professionals, podcasts focused on personal development and self-improvement can be a goldmine of inspiration and motivation. These podcasts often delve into topics such as overcoming creative blocks, finding your unique voice, and maintaining a healthy mindset in the competitive music industry. Sports enthusiasts and professionals can also find immense value in mental health and well-being podcasts. These podcasts offer insights into the psychological aspects of sports performance, such as visualization techniques, goal setting, and mental toughness. Listening to these podcasts can help athletes and sports enthusiasts enhance their mental game and achieve peak performance.

Film graduates and professionals can benefit from mental health and well-being podcasts that focus on the unique challenges of the film industry. These podcasts often touch on topics such as dealing with rejection, managing stress on set, and maintaining a healthy work-life balance in a demanding industry.

In addition to these specific niches, mental health and well-being podcasts cater to a wide range of interests, including technology and innovation, comedy and entertainment, travel and adventure, and more. No matter your niche or interest, there is a mental health and well-being podcast out there that can provide you with valuable insights and support.

As you delve into mental health and well-being podcasts, keep in mind that they are not a substitute for professional help. If you are experiencing severe mental health issues, it is important to seek help from a licensed therapist or counselor.

In conclusion, mental health and well-being podcasts offer a wealth of knowledge and support for individuals from various fields and interests. By incorporating these podcasts into your daily routine, you can gain valuable insights, strategies, and inspiration to enhance your mental well-being and achieve personal and professional success. So, grab your headphones and start delving into the world of mental health and well-being podcasts today!

Learning from Experts in Various Fields

In the world of podcasting, knowledge is power. Aspiring podcasters in 2024 have a unique opportunity to tap into the vast expertise of professionals from various fields. Whether you're an entrepreneur seeking advice, a music professional looking for inspiration, or a sports enthusiast wanting to dive deeper into your favorite games, podcasting can connect you with experts who can share their wisdom and insights.

One of the greatest advantages of starting a podcast in 2024 is the ability to learn from experts in your niche. Entrepreneurs will find a wealth of knowledge waiting to be explored through podcasts focused on personal development and self-improvement. These podcasts can provide valuable insights into business strategies, leadership skills, and the mindset needed for success. By listening to successful entrepreneurs, you can gain valuable tips and tricks to apply to your own ventures.

For those interested in health and wellness, there are podcasts dedicated to providing the latest research, trends, and tips for living a healthier life. Technology and innovation podcasts can keep you up to date on the latest tech advancements and how they can impact your industry. Aspiring musicians can find inspiration and guidance from music professionals who share their experiences and offer valuable advice on navigating the music industry.

Sports enthusiasts will also find a treasure trove of podcasts dedicated to their favorite games. From in-depth analysis of matches to interviews with sports professionals, these podcasts provide a deeper understanding of the sports world. Film graduates and professionals can gain insights from industry veterans who share their experiences and offer tips on breaking into the competitive world of film.

No matter your niche, there are comedy and entertainment podcasts that can brighten your day and provide a much-needed escape from the daily grind. Travel and adventure podcasts can transport you to far-off destinations and inspire your next adventure.

In conclusion, starting a podcast in 2024 opens up a world of learning opportunities from experts in various fields. Entrepreneurs, business professionals, music professionals, sports enthusiasts, film graduates, and more can all benefit from the insights and wisdom shared through podcasts. Whether you're looking to start a podcast, explore personal development, improve your health and wellness, stay informed about the latest technology, find inspiration for your creative pursuits, or simply enjoy some entertainment, there's a podcast out there for you. So, tune in, learn, and let the experts guide you on your journey to success.

Cultivating Positive Habits through Podcasting

In today's fast-paced world, where personal and professional lives can often collide, it is essential to find effective ways to cultivate positive habits that contribute to our overall growth and success. One powerful tool that has gained immense popularity in recent years is podcasting. With its ability to provide on-the-go learning and entertainment, podcasting has become a go-to platform for entrepreneurs, business professionals, music professionals, sports enthusiasts, musicians, film graduates, and many more.

Start a podcast in 2024: Aspiring entrepreneurs looking to venture into the world of podcasting can utilize this subchapter to gain valuable insights on how to start their podcast successfully. From choosing the right equipment and software to understanding the importance of content planning and promotion, this subchapter covers everything entrepreneurs need to know to launch a podcast that resonates with their target audience.

Podcasts focused on personal development and self-improvement: For individuals seeking personal growth and self-improvement, podcasting offers a wealth of resources. This subchapter highlights the best podcasts in this niche, providing recommendations that cover topics such as goal setting, time management, mindset, and motivation. Listeners can gain practical tips and strategies to cultivate positive habits and transform their lives.

Health and wellness podcasts: With an increasing focus on well-being, health, and fitness, podcasting has become a popular medium for professionals and enthusiasts in the health and wellness industry. This subchapter explores a range of podcasts that delve into nutrition, exercise, mental health, mindfulness, and overall well-being. Listeners can discover expert insights, inspiring stories, and practical advice to cultivate a healthier lifestyle.

Technology and innovation podcasts: In an era driven by technological advancements, staying updated with the latest trends and innovations is crucial for professionals across industries. This subchapter highlights podcasts that delve into cutting-edge technologies, industry trends, and futuristic ideas. Listeners can gain knowledge and inspiration from experts in the field, fostering a mindset of continuous learning and innovation.

Comedy and entertainment podcasts: Laughter is the best medicine, and comedy and entertainment podcasts provide the perfect dose of it. This subchapter showcases podcasts that offer light-hearted content, hilarious stories, and entertaining conversations. By incorporating humor and entertainment into their daily routines, entrepreneurs, business professionals, and other individuals can cultivate a positive mindset and alleviate stress.

Podcasts about travel and adventure: For those with a passion for travel and adventure, this subchapter presents an array of podcasts that transport listeners to exciting destinations and inspire them to embark on their own journeys. From travel tips and destination guides to inspiring travel stories, these podcasts serve as a source of inspiration and motivation for individuals seeking new experiences. Podcasts for sports enthusiasts: Sports enthusiasts can dive into this subchapter to find podcasts that cater to their passion. Whether it's discussions on the latest sports news, insights from athletes and coaches, or analysis of game strategies, these podcasts offer a platform for sports enthusiasts to stay connected with their favorite sports and cultivate a deeper understanding and appreciation for the games they love.

By leveraging the power of podcasting, entrepreneurs, business professionals, music professionals, sports enthusiasts, musicians, film graduates, and film professionals can cultivate positive habits that contribute to their personal and professional growth. Whether it's starting a podcast, focusing on personal development, exploring health and wellness, staying updated with technology, seeking entertainment, embracing travel and adventure, or immersing in the world of sports, podcasting offers a versatile platform to cultivate positive habits and enhance one's overall well-being.

Chapter 10: Health and Wellness Podcasts

Exploring Fitness and Exercise Podcasts

In recent years, podcasts have emerged as a popular medium for consuming information and entertainment on the go. With their convenience and accessibility, it's no wonder that podcasting has become a powerful tool for entrepreneurs, business professionals, music professionals, sports enthusiasts, and more. If you're interested in starting your own podcast or simply looking for new content to listen to, exploring fitness and exercise podcasts can provide you with valuable insights, motivation, and inspiration.

For aspiring entrepreneurs, podcasts offer a wealth of knowledge on business strategies, marketing techniques, and success stories from industry leaders. Tune in to podcasts like "The Startup Life" or "Entrepreneur on Fire" to gain practical tips and learn from the experiences of successful entrepreneurs. These podcasts can help you navigate the challenges of starting and growing your own business.

If you're focused on personal development and self-improvement, there are podcasts tailored specifically to help you achieve your goals. Shows like "The Tony Robbins Podcast" or "The School of Greatness" provide guidance on overcoming obstacles, building self-confidence, and achieving personal success. Whether you're looking to improve your mindset, boost your productivity, or enhance your overall well-being, these podcasts offer valuable insights and actionable advice.

For those interested in health and wellness, fitness and exercise podcasts are a treasure trove of information. From workout routines and nutrition tips to mental health and mindfulness practices, podcasts like "The Model Health Show" or "The Rich Roll Podcast" cover a wide range of topics to help you live a healthier and more balanced life. Whether you're a fitness enthusiast or just starting your wellness journey, these podcasts can provide you with the guidance and motivation you need to stay on track.

Technology and innovation podcasts can also offer valuable insights for entrepreneurs and business professionals. Shows like "The Tim Ferriss Show" or "Masters of Scale" explore the latest trends in technology, innovation, and entrepreneurship. These podcasts dive deep into the minds of industry leaders, providing you with valuable lessons and strategies to stay ahead in an ever-evolving business landscape.

If you're looking for some light-hearted entertainment, comedy and entertainment podcasts can provide a much-needed break from your daily routine. Shows like "The Joe Rogan Experience" or "Conan O'Brien Needs a Friend" feature interviews with celebrities and comedians, offering a blend of laughter and interesting conversations.

For sports enthusiasts, podcasts dedicated to sports provide in-depth analysis, interviews with athletes, and discussions on the latest news and trends in the sports world. Whether you're a fan of basketball, football, soccer, or any other sport, podcasts like "The Bill Simmons Podcast" or "The Lowe Post" offer engaging content that will keep you informed and entertained.

So, whether you're looking to start your own podcast, seeking inspiration for personal development, or simply interested in staying fit and healthy, exploring fitness and exercise podcasts can be a valuable addition to your podcasting journey. With a wide range of topics and perspectives to choose from, there's something for everyone in the world of fitness and exercise podcasts.

Nutrition and Healthy Eating Podcasts

In today's fast-paced world, maintaining a healthy lifestyle can be challenging. With hectic schedules and endless responsibilities, it's easy to neglect our nutrition and fall into unhealthy eating habits. However, thanks to the power of podcasting, entrepreneurs, business professionals, music professionals, sports enthusiasts, and individuals from various niches now have access to a wealth of information on nutrition and healthy eating.

"Podcasting 2024: A Step-by-Step Guide to Starting Your Own Podcast" recognizes the importance of a healthy lifestyle and the role that nutrition plays in overall well-being. This subchapter focuses on introducing the audience to the world of nutrition and healthy eating podcasts, providing recommendations and insights for those interested in this niche.

Start a podcast in 2024? Why not consider a nutrition and healthy eating podcast! With the rising global interest in health and wellness, entrepreneurs and business professionals can tap into this niche and offer valuable content to their audience. From discussing the latest trends in nutrition to sharing delicious and nutritious recipes, a nutrition podcast can attract a dedicated following.

Podcasts for aspiring entrepreneurs can benefit from exploring the topic of nutrition and healthy eating. By emphasizing the importance of a balanced diet and its impact on productivity and success, these podcasts can provide valuable insights for entrepreneurs looking to optimize their performance.

Personal development and self-improvement are popular niches in the podcasting world. A podcast focused on nutrition and healthy eating can contribute to personal growth by educating listeners on the benefits of proper nutrition, guiding them towards making healthier choices, and empowering them to take control of their overall well-being.

For those interested in health and wellness, technology and innovation podcasts can explore the latest advancements in nutrition science and technology. These podcasts can discuss topics such as food tracking apps, wearable devices, and personalized nutrition, offering listeners practical tools to enhance their healthy eating journey.

Incorporating humor and entertainment into nutrition and healthy eating podcasts can make the topic more approachable and enjoyable. Comedy and entertainment podcasts can explore the lighter side of nutrition, debunking myths and sharing funny anecdotes about the challenges of maintaining a healthy diet. Podcasts about travel and adventure can also incorporate nutrition and healthy eating as they explore different cuisines and food cultures around the world. These podcasts can provide valuable insights into how to maintain a healthy diet while traveling and inspire listeners to explore new culinary experiences.

Lastly, sports enthusiasts can benefit from podcasts that focus on nutrition and its impact on athletic performance. These podcasts can delve into topics such as sports nutrition, pre and post-workout meals, and supplements, offering valuable information for individuals looking to optimize their sports performance.

In conclusion, the subchapter "Nutrition and Healthy Eating Podcasts" in "Podcasting 2024: A Step-by-Step Guide to Starting Your Own Podcast" highlights the importance of nutrition and healthy eating in today's fast-paced world. By exploring this niche, entrepreneurs, business professionals, music professionals, sports enthusiasts, and individuals from various niches can provide valuable content to their audience, contribute to personal development, and inspire healthier lifestyles. Whether it's starting a podcast dedicated to nutrition, incorporating nutrition into existing podcast themes, or simply tuning in to existing nutrition and healthy eating podcasts, there are endless opportunities to explore this exciting and vital topic.

Mental Health and Self-Care Podcasts

In today's fast-paced and demanding world, it's more important than ever to prioritize mental health and self-care. As entrepreneurs, business professionals, music professionals, sports enthusiasts, musicians, film graduates, and professionals, we often find ourselves constantly on the go, juggling multiple responsibilities and facing high levels of stress. That's why incorporating mental health and self-care practices into our daily lives is crucial for our overall well-being.

One powerful tool that has gained immense popularity in recent years is podcasts. Podcasts offer a convenient and accessible way to access valuable information, guidance, and support on various topics, including mental health and self-care. Whether you're looking for advice on managing stress, improving your mindset, or finding practical strategies to enhance your well-being, there is a wide range of podcasts available to cater to your specific needs.

For aspiring entrepreneurs, podcasts focused on personal development and self-improvement can be a game-changer. These podcasts provide insights from successful business leaders, industry experts, and thought leaders who share their stories, experiences, and practical advice on building a thriving business while maintaining a healthy work-life balance.

Health and wellness podcasts offer a wealth of information on various aspects of mental health, self-care practices, and overall well-being. From mindfulness and meditation to nutrition and exercise, these podcasts provide valuable tips and techniques to help you prioritize your mental health and take care of yourself.

Technology and innovation podcasts delve into the latest advancements in mental health technologies, apps, and tools that can support your self-care journey. These podcasts keep you updated on the latest trends and provide recommendations on how to leverage technology to enhance your mental well-being.

While self-care is essential, so is laughter and entertainment. Comedy and entertainment podcasts offer a much-needed break from the stress and pressures of everyday life. Laughing not only lifts your mood but also has numerous health benefits, making it an integral part of self-care.

For sports enthusiasts, podcasts about travel and adventure can provide inspiration and motivation to explore the world and engage in physical activities that promote mental well-being. These podcasts share stories of athletes, adventurers, and explorers who have overcome challenges and found fulfillment through their pursuit of adventure.

In conclusion, mental health and self-care podcasts are a valuable resource for entrepreneurs, business professionals, music professionals, sports enthusiasts, musicians, film graduates, and professionals. They offer practical advice, inspiration, and support on various aspects of mental health, self-care, personal development, and overall well-being. By incorporating these podcasts into your daily routine, you can prioritize your mental health and well-being, leading to increased productivity, resilience, and fulfillment in both your personal and professional life.

Alternative Medicine and Holistic Healing Podcasts

In recent years, there has been a growing interest in alternative medicine and holistic healing practices. People are seeking natural and holistic approaches to their health and wellness, and podcasts have become a popular medium for sharing knowledge and experiences in this field. Whether you are an entrepreneur, business professional, music enthusiast, sports professional, or simply someone interested in personal development and self-improvement, there are plenty of podcasts out there that cater to your interests.

If you are looking to start a podcast in 2024, exploring the alternative medicine and holistic healing niche can be a great choice. This subchapter will guide you through the process of creating a podcast dedicated to this topic, from brainstorming ideas to recording and editing episodes. You will learn how to research and choose the right guests, create engaging content, and promote your podcast to reach a wider audience.

For aspiring entrepreneurs, podcasts focused on personal development and self-improvement can provide valuable insights and inspiration. These podcasts often feature interviews with successful entrepreneurs, experts in various fields, and individuals who have overcome challenges and achieved personal growth. By listening to these podcasts, you can gain practical tips and strategies to help you navigate the business world and achieve your goals.

Health and wellness podcasts are not only informative but also offer practical advice and tips for maintaining a balanced and healthy lifestyle. From discussions on nutrition and exercise to exploring different alternative medicine practices, these podcasts provide a wealth of information for those seeking to improve their physical and mental well-being.

Technology and innovation podcasts can also be relevant to the alternative medicine and holistic healing niche. As technology continues to advance, new tools and applications are being developed to support these practices. Podcasts in this category explore the latest trends and innovations in the field, discussing how technology can enhance the effectiveness of alternative medicine and holistic healing.

For those seeking entertainment and laughter, comedy and entertainment podcasts can provide a refreshing break from the daily grind. These podcasts often feature comedians and entertainers discussing various topics, including alternative medicine and holistic healing, in a light-hearted and humorous manner.

If you are a sports enthusiast or professional, podcasts about travel and adventure can be an excellent source of inspiration. These podcasts often feature athletes and adventurers discussing their experiences and offering insights on how they maintain their physical and mental well-being while pursuing their passions.

In conclusion, alternative medicine and holistic healing podcasts cater to a wide range of interests and niches. Whether you are looking to start a podcast in 2024, seeking personal development and self-improvement, exploring health and wellness, staying up-to-date with technology and innovation, or simply wanting to be entertained, there is a podcast out there for you. Take the time to explore the vast world of alternative medicine and holistic healing podcasts and discover new perspectives, insights, and inspiration for a well-rounded and fulfilling life.

Chapter 11: Technology and Innovation Podcasts

Staying Updated on the Latest Tech Trends

In today's fast-paced world, staying updated on the latest tech trends is crucial for entrepreneurs, business professionals, and individuals in various industries such as music, sports, film, and more. As technology continues to evolve rapidly, it is essential to keep up with the latest advancements to remain competitive and relevant in your field. This subchapter will provide valuable insights and tips on how to stay informed about the latest tech trends and leverage them to enhance your podcasting journey.

Start a podcast in 2024:

If you are considering starting your own podcast in 2024, it is crucial to stay updated on the latest tech trends. From new podcasting platforms to innovative recording equipment and editing software, the podcasting landscape is continually evolving. By staying informed, you can make informed decisions about the tools and resources you need to launch a successful podcast in the current year.

Podcasts for aspiring entrepreneurs:

Entrepreneurs are always on the lookout for the latest trends and ideas to drive their businesses forward. By listening to podcasts focused on entrepreneurship, you can gain valuable insights from industry experts, successful entrepreneurs, and thought leaders. These podcasts often cover topics such as business strategies, marketing techniques, financial management, and emerging technologies that can help aspiring entrepreneurs stay ahead of the curve.

Podcasts focused on personal development and self-improvement:

For individuals looking to enhance their personal growth and self-improvement, podcasts dedicated to personal development can be an invaluable resource. These podcasts cover topics such as mindfulness, productivity hacks, goal setting, and mental health. By staying updated on the latest trends in personal development, you can acquire new skills, improve your mindset, and unlock your full potential.

Health and wellness podcasts:

In the fast-paced world we live in, health and wellness have become increasingly important. Health and wellness podcasts offer valuable insights into exercise routines, nutrition, mental well-being, and overall lifestyle choices. By staying updated on the latest tech trends in the health and wellness industry, you can discover new tools, apps, and devices that can help you live a healthier and more balanced life.

Technology and innovation podcasts:

To stay ahead in any industry, it is crucial to stay informed about the latest technological advancements. Technology and innovation podcasts provide updates on emerging technologies, breakthrough inventions, and how they impact various sectors. By listening to these podcasts, you can gain a competitive edge by implementing the latest tech trends into your podcasting journey.

Comedy and entertainment podcasts:

For those looking for a lighter side of podcasting, comedy and entertainment podcasts offer a welcome escape. These podcasts cover topics such as stand-up comedy, celebrity interviews, pop culture, and more. By staying updated on the latest tech trends in the comedy and entertainment industry, you can discover new ways to engage your audience, explore innovative storytelling techniques, and create content that resonates with your listeners.

Podcasts about travel and adventure:

If you are a travel enthusiast or looking for inspiration for your next adventure, podcasts dedicated to travel and adventure can be your go-to resource. These podcasts cover topics such as destination guides, travel tips, adventure stories, and cultural experiences. By staying updated on the latest tech trends in the travel industry, you can explore new tools, apps, and platforms that can enhance your travel experiences and share them with your audience.

Podcasts for sports enthusiasts:

Sports enthusiasts can stay updated on the latest tech trends in the sports industry by listening to podcasts dedicated to sports. These podcasts cover topics such as sports analysis, athlete interviews, game predictions, and sports business insights. By staying informed about the latest tech trends, you can discover new ways to engage with your audience, leverage data analytics, and enhance your sports-related content.

In conclusion, staying updated on the latest tech trends is essential for entrepreneurs, business professionals, music professionals, sports enthusiasts, musicians, film graduates, and professionals in various industries. By staying informed about the latest advancements, you can make informed decisions, stay competitive, and create content that resonates with your target audience. Whether you are starting a podcast in 2024, seeking personal development resources, exploring health and wellness trends, or diving into the world of technology and innovation, staying updated on the latest tech trends is a valuable asset for your podcasting journey.

Exploring Artificial Intelligence and Machine Learning

In today's rapidly evolving digital landscape, it is impossible to ignore the impact of artificial intelligence (AI) and machine learning (ML) on various industries. From healthcare to entertainment, AI and ML technologies are revolutionizing how we live, work, and interact. This subchapter titled "Exploring Artificial Intelligence and Machine Learning" delves deep into the world of AI and ML, specifically focusing on their potential applications in the podcasting industry.

For entrepreneurs and business professionals, understanding the potential of AI and ML can unlock limitless possibilities for their podcasting ventures. By leveraging AI-powered algorithms, podcasters can enhance their content discovery, personalize listener experiences, and optimize monetization strategies. This subchapter will provide practical insights and strategies for integrating AI and ML into podcasting workflows, helping entrepreneurs stay ahead of the curve in the ever-competitive podcasting landscape.

For music professionals, the rise of AI and ML presents both opportunities and challenges. AI-generated music, virtual artists, and personalized music recommendations are reshaping the music industry. This subchapter will explore how musicians can leverage AI and ML to create unique podcast soundtracks, engage with fans on a deeper level, and explore new revenue streams.

Sports enthusiasts and professionals, on the other hand, can benefit from AI and ML technologies in various ways. From predictive analytics for sports betting to player performance analysis, AI and ML algorithms are transforming how we consume and analyze sports-related content. This subchapter will delve into the world of AI-powered sports podcasting, exploring how sports enthusiasts can leverage these technologies to deliver engaging, data-driven content to their listeners.

For film graduates and professionals, the integration of AI and ML in podcasting opens up exciting possibilities for storytelling and audience engagement. This subchapter will shed light on how AI-generated scripts, voice recognition technologies, and immersive audio experiences can enhance the podcasting experience for film enthusiasts and professionals.

In conclusion, this subchapter aims to provide entrepreneurs, business professionals, music professionals, sports enthusiasts, film graduates, and professionals with a comprehensive understanding of how AI and ML are shaping the podcasting landscape. By exploring potential applications in various niches such as personal development, health and wellness, technology and innovation, comedy and entertainment, travel and adventure, and sports, readers will gain valuable insights to start or enhance their podcasting journey in 2024 and beyond.

Understanding Blockchain and Cryptocurrency

In today's rapidly evolving digital landscape, it is crucial for entrepreneurs, business professionals, music professionals, sports enthusiasts, musicians, film graduates, and professionals alike to grasp the fundamental concepts of blockchain and cryptocurrency. As these technologies continue to revolutionize various industries, including podcasting, it is essential to have a solid understanding of their potential and how they can be leveraged to stay ahead of the curve.

Blockchain, at its core, is a decentralized ledger that records transactions across multiple computers. Its transparent and tamper-proof nature makes it an ideal solution for various applications, from financial transactions to supply chain management and beyond. By understanding the underlying mechanisms of blockchain, entrepreneurs can explore innovative ways to enhance security, transparency, and efficiency within their podcasts.

Cryptocurrency, on the other hand, is a digital or virtual form of currency that utilizes cryptography for secure transactions. Bitcoin, the most well-known cryptocurrency, is just the tip of the iceberg. Aspiring entrepreneurs can explore the potential of creating their own cryptocurrencies or accept existing ones as a form of payment for their podcasting services. Additionally, understanding cryptocurrency can open doors to investment opportunities and partnerships within the digital economy.

For podcasters focused on personal development and self-improvement, blockchain can offer a new level of credibility and accountability. By recording podcast episodes and interactions on the blockchain, listeners can verify the authenticity of the content, building trust and loyalty. Implementing cryptocurrency rewards or micropayments for valuable insights or exclusive content can also incentivize listeners to engage more actively with the podcast.

Health and wellness podcasts can benefit from blockchain's ability to securely store and share sensitive medical information. By integrating blockchain technology into their podcasts, hosts can offer personalized health recommendations, track progress, and connect with professionals in the industry. This secure and transparent ecosystem can empower listeners to take control of their well-being.

Technology and innovation podcasts can delve into the intricate workings of blockchain and cryptocurrency, exploring the latest advancements, trends, and potential disruptions. By keeping the audience informed about emerging technologies and their implications, these podcasts can become a valuable resource for entrepreneurs and professionals seeking to leverage these tools effectively.

Comedy and entertainment podcasts can tap into the fun and creative side of blockchain and cryptocurrency. Exploring the lighter aspects, hosts can discuss the rise of meme coins, the influence of social media on digital currencies, and the potential for blockchain-based gaming. By infusing humor and entertainment into the discussion, these podcasts can engage a wider audience and make complex concepts more accessible.

For sports enthusiasts, blockchain and cryptocurrency offer exciting opportunities. Podcasts can explore the use of blockchain in sports betting, ticket sales, and the trading of collectibles. Additionally, hosts can discuss the rise of fan tokens, allowing supporters to have a direct impact on their favorite teams' decisions. By understanding these technologies, sports enthusiasts can stay ahead of the game and participate actively in the evolving sports industry.

In conclusion, understanding blockchain and cryptocurrency is crucial for entrepreneurs, business professionals, music professionals, sports enthusiasts, musicians, film graduates, and professionals in various niches of podcasting. By embracing these technologies, podcasters can enhance security, transparency, credibility, and audience engagement. Whether you're starting a podcast in 2024, focusing on personal development, health and wellness, technology and innovation, comedy and entertainment, travel and adventure, or sports, blockchain and cryptocurrency offer endless possibilities to explore and thrive in the digital era.

Innovations in Virtual Reality and Augmented Reality

As we dive into the future of podcasting in 2024, it's essential to explore the latest advancements that technology has to offer. One such area that holds tremendous potential for podcasters is the realm of virtual reality (VR) and augmented reality (AR). These innovative technologies have the power to revolutionize the way we consume and engage with podcasts, offering exciting new possibilities for entrepreneurs, business professionals, music enthusiasts, sports professionals, and more.

Imagine being transported to a virtual studio where you can interact with your favorite podcast host as if they were right beside you. With VR, podcasters can create immersive experiences that blur the line between reality and digital content. Listeners can feel like they're part of a live recording, with the ability to explore the virtual environment and engage with other listeners in real-time. This opens up a whole new level of engagement and intimacy for podcast creators and their audiences.

AR, on the other hand, allows podcasters to overlay digital information onto the real world, creating a truly interactive experience. Imagine listening to a travel podcast while exploring a new city, and with the help of AR, you can see relevant information, historical facts, and even virtual tour guides popping up on your smartphone or AR glasses. This technology can also be applied to sports podcasts, where listeners can visualize game statistics and player information in real-time while watching a live match.

For musicians and film professionals, VR and AR offer exciting possibilities for immersive storytelling. Imagine creating a podcast where listeners can step into a virtual concert hall and experience a live performance as if they were there in person. Or imagine a film podcast where listeners can watch trailers and exclusive behind-the-scenes footage in AR, enhancing their understanding and appreciation of the craft.

Health and wellness podcasts can also benefit from these technologies, offering guided meditation experiences in VR or providing visual cues and instructions for workout routines in AR. The possibilities are endless, and it's up to entrepreneurs and podcasters to harness the power of VR and AR to create unique and engaging content for their audience.

As we look ahead to the future of podcasting, it's clear that VR and AR will play a significant role in transforming the way we consume and engage with audio content. Whether you're interested in starting a podcast in 2024, focusing on personal development, health and wellness, technology and innovation, comedy, travel, or sports, incorporating VR and AR into your podcasting strategy can elevate your content and provide a truly immersive experience for your listeners. The future is here, and it's time to embrace the innovations in virtual reality and augmented reality for a truly unforgettable podcasting journey.

Chapter 12: Comedy and Entertainment Podcasts

Exploring Different Comedy Podcast Formats

Comedy and entertainment podcasts have gained tremendous popularity in recent years, providing a much-needed escape from the daily grind and allowing listeners to laugh and unwind. If you are considering starting your own comedy podcast, it's essential to understand the various formats available to you. This subchapter will explore the different comedy podcast formats and help you choose the one that best suits your style and audience.

1. Solo Comedy Podcast:

A solo comedy podcast involves a single host delivering funny monologues, sharing anecdotes, or performing comedic sketches. This format allows for complete creative control and is ideal for individuals who excel at delivering humor on their own.

2. Panel or Roundtable Discussion:

In this format, a group of comedians or entertainment professionals come together to discuss humorous topics, share stories, and engage in witty banter. This format works well for podcasts with a diverse range of perspectives and comedic styles.

3. Interview-Style Comedy Podcast:

Similar to traditional interview podcasts, this format features a host interviewing comedians or celebrities, discussing their careers, sharing funny stories, and exploring their unique comedic processes. This format allows for a more in-depth look into the world of comedy.

4. Improv Comedy Podcast:

Improv comedy podcasts are unscripted and rely on spontaneous jokes, skits, and improvisation. This format requires quick thinking, wit, and the ability to bounce off other comedians. It provides an authentic and unpredictable comedic experience for listeners.

5. Narrative Comedy Podcast:

Narrative comedy podcasts tell fictional stories using comedy as a primary tool. This format combines humor with storytelling, allowing for the creation of engaging characters, intriguing plots, and hilarious situations. It is ideal for individuals with a flair for writing and storytelling.

No matter which format you choose, it's crucial to consider your target audience and their preferences. Entrepreneurs, business professionals, sports enthusiasts, and more all have unique tastes in comedy. Tailoring your content to their interests will ensure a loyal following.

Additionally, you may want to consider incorporating elements from other niches, such as personal development or technology, to appeal to a wider audience. For example, a comedy podcast focused on personal development could provide hilarious insights into overcoming challenges in life and business.

Remember, the success of your comedy podcast depends on your ability to entertain, engage, and connect with your audience. Experiment with different formats, stay true to your comedic style, and most importantly, have fun with it. Happy podcasting!

Analyzing Successful Comedy Podcasts

Comedy podcasts have become increasingly popular over the past decade, offering a unique blend of entertainment, humor, and insightful discussions. In this subchapter, we will delve into the world of successful comedy podcasts and analyze the key factors that contribute to their popularity and longevity. Whether you are an aspiring podcaster, business professional, or simply a comedy enthusiast, understanding the strategies behind successful comedy podcasts can provide valuable insights into creating your own engaging content.

When it comes to comedy podcasts, one of the most important aspects to consider is the chemistry between the hosts. Successful comedy podcasts often feature a dynamic duo or a group of hosts with a great rapport and comedic timing. This chemistry is crucial in creating a relaxed and conversational atmosphere that resonates with the audience. It allows for organic banter and seamless transitions between jokes and topics.

Another key factor in analyzing successful comedy podcasts is the quality of the content. While humor is at the forefront, it is essential to strike a balance between entertainment and substance. The best comedy podcasts often infuse their humor with insightful discussions, personal anecdotes, and thought-provoking commentary. This combination keeps the audience engaged and coming back for more.

Successful comedy podcasts also understand the importance of regularity and consistency. They maintain a consistent publishing schedule, ensuring that their audience knows when to expect new episodes. Additionally, they leverage social media platforms to engage with their audience, share updates, and create a sense of community. By nurturing this online presence, successful comedy podcasts cultivate a loyal fan base that actively participates in discussions and promotes their content.

Furthermore, innovation and adaptability play a significant role in the success of comedy podcasts. The most successful podcasts understand the evolving trends and preferences of their target audience. They continuously experiment with new formats, invite guest comedians, and explore different topics to keep their content fresh and captivating.

In conclusion, analyzing successful comedy podcasts provides valuable insights for anyone interested in starting their own podcast or understanding the key factors behind engaging and entertaining content. By focusing on building chemistry between hosts, maintaining a high-quality content, consistency, and embracing innovation, aspiring podcasters can create their own unique brand of comedy that resonates with their audience. Whether you are an entrepreneur, business professional, or simply a comedy enthusiast, the world of comedy podcasts offers an abundance of inspiration and entertainment.

Creating Engaging and Funny Content

In the world of podcasting, there is one golden rule that every podcaster should follow: create engaging and funny content. Whether you are starting a podcast in 2024, targeting aspiring entrepreneurs, or focusing on personal development and self-improvement, the key to success lies in capturing your audience's attention and keeping them entertained. This subchapter will provide you with valuable tips and tricks on how to create content that is both engaging and funny, regardless of the niche you are targeting.

To begin with, it is important to understand your audience. Entrepreneurs, business professionals, music professionals, sports enthusiasts, and other niche audiences all have different tastes and preferences. Take the time to research and understand what makes your target audience tick. What are their pain points? What kind of humor resonates with them? By understanding your audience, you can tailor your content to their specific needs and preferences.

Once you have a clear understanding of your audience, it's time to brainstorm ideas for engaging and funny content. Consider incorporating humor into your podcast episodes through storytelling, anecdotes, or even skits. Injecting humor into your content not only keeps your audience entertained but also helps to build a connection with them. People love to laugh, and by making them laugh, you create a memorable and enjoyable experience.

Additionally, consider inviting guests who have a knack for humor or have a unique perspective on your podcast's topic. By bringing in fresh voices and different personalities, you add variety and enhance the entertainment value of your episodes. Your guests can share funny anecdotes, provide comedic relief, or engage in lighthearted banter with you, making your podcast more engaging and enjoyable for your listeners.

Incorporating humor is not limited to the spoken content of your podcast. You can also experiment with funny episode titles, witty descriptions, and engaging cover art that catches the eye. Remember, the goal is to stand out in a sea of podcasts and attract your audience's attention.

Finally, encourage audience participation and engagement. Ask for their feedback, questions, or funny stories related to your podcast's topic. This not only creates a sense of community but also provides you with an opportunity to incorporate their contributions into future episodes, making them feel involved and invested in your podcast.

In conclusion, creating engaging and funny content is essential for any successful podcast. Regardless of your niche, understanding your audience, brainstorming creative ideas, inviting guests, and encouraging audience participation will help you create content that keeps your listeners entertained and coming back for more. So, let your creativity run wild, inject humor into your podcast, and watch your audience grow.

Utilizing Humor to Connect with Your Audience

In the world of podcasting, connecting with your audience is key to building a loyal and engaged following. One powerful tool that can help you achieve this is humor. Incorporating humor into your podcast not only entertains your listeners but also creates a sense of connection and relatability. In this subchapter, we will explore the benefits of using humor and how you can effectively incorporate it into your podcast episodes.

Why Use Humor?

Humor has the ability to break down barriers and create a positive and engaging atmosphere. It can make your podcast more enjoyable to listen to and keep your audience coming back for more. When used appropriately, humor can also help you convey complex information in a more digestible and memorable way.

Connecting with Different Audiences

Entrepreneurs, business professionals, music professionals, sports enthusiasts, musicians, film graduates, and professionals, to name a few, all have different interests and backgrounds. However, one thing that unites them is the universal appeal of humor. Utilizing humor in your podcast can bridge the gap between various niches and create a common ground for your diverse audience.

How to Incorporate Humor into Your Podcast

1. Tell Funny Anecdotes: Share personal stories or experiences that are relatable and humorous. This will not only entertain your audience but also make you more relatable as a host.

2. Use Funny Segments: Incorporate recurring segments in your podcast that are light-hearted and humorous. This can be a funny news roundup, listener-submitted jokes, or a comedy skit.

3. Interview Comedians: Invite comedians or funny personalities as guests on your podcast. Their humor and wit will add an extra element of entertainment and engagement to your episodes.

4. Inject Humor in Scripts: If you script your podcast episodes, make sure to include jokes, puns, or funny one-liners throughout. This will keep your content engaging and entertaining.

5. Embrace Improvisation: Be open to spontaneity and embrace unexpected funny moments during your podcast recordings. Sometimes, the best humor comes from unscripted banter and natural wit.

Remember, humor should always be used with sensitivity and respect for your audience. What might be funny to one person could be offensive to another. Stay true to your podcast's tone and audience, and always be mindful of the impact your humor may have.

By utilizing humor effectively, you can create a podcast that not only educates and informs but also entertains and connects with your audience. Whether you're starting a podcast in 2024 or focusing on personal development, health and wellness, technology and innovation, comedy and entertainment, sports, or travel and adventure, humor can be a powerful tool to engage your listeners and build a strong community around your podcast.

Chapter 13: Podcasts about Travel and Adventure

Sharing Travel Experiences and Tips

In this subchapter, we will delve into the exciting world of sharing travel experiences and tips through podcasting. Whether you are an entrepreneur, business professional, music enthusiast, sports professional, or a film graduate, this chapter is designed to help you tap into the growing niche of travel and adventure podcasts.

Start a podcast in 2024:

With the podcasting industry booming, starting your own podcast has become more accessible than ever before. We will guide you through the step-by-step process of launching your travel podcast in 2024, from conceptualizing the theme to recording and editing your episodes. By the end of this chapter, you will have the knowledge and tools to confidently share your own travel experiences and tips with the world.

Podcasts for aspiring entrepreneurs:

Travel can be a great source of inspiration for entrepreneurs, and this subchapter will explore how you can use your travel experiences to provide valuable insights and lessons for aspiring entrepreneurs. We will discuss how to incorporate business advice and strategies into your travel podcast, creating a unique and valuable resource for entrepreneurs looking to start their own ventures.

Podcasts focused on personal development and self-improvement: Traveling often leads to personal growth and self-discovery. In this section, we will explore how you can create a travel podcast that focuses on personal development and self-improvement. We will discuss topics such as overcoming challenges, stepping out of your comfort zone, and the transformative power of travel. By sharing your own experiences and tips, you can inspire and motivate your listeners to embark on their own personal journeys.

Health and wellness podcasts:

Traveling offers endless opportunities to explore different wellness practices and lifestyles. In this subchapter, we will explore how you can incorporate health and wellness themes into your travel podcast. We will discuss topics such as mindfulness, fitness, nutrition, and alternative healing practices. By sharing your own experiences and tips, you can provide valuable insights to help your listeners maintain their well-being while traveling.

Technology and innovation podcasts:

The travel industry is constantly evolving, thanks to technological advancements and innovative ideas. In this section, we will explore how you can create a travel podcast that focuses on technology and innovation in the travel industry. We will discuss topics such as travel apps, virtual reality experiences, and sustainable travel solutions. By sharing the latest trends and innovations, you can keep your listeners informed and inspired.

Comedy and entertainment podcasts:

Traveling often leads to funny and entertaining stories. In this subchapter, we will explore how you can create a travel podcast that focuses on comedy and entertainment. We will discuss storytelling techniques, improvisation, and incorporating humor into your episodes. By sharing your own humorous travel anecdotes and tips, you can provide your listeners with a light-hearted and entertaining experience.

Podcasts about travel and adventure:

In this subchapter, we will delve into the specifics of creating a travel and adventure podcast. We will discuss topics such as choosing destinations, planning itineraries, and engaging with local cultures. By sharing your own travel experiences and tips, you can inspire your listeners to embark on their own adventures and explore the world.

Podcasts for sports enthusiasts:

Sports and travel often go hand in hand, and in this section, we will explore how you can create a travel podcast that caters to sports enthusiasts. We will discuss topics such as attending major sporting events, exploring sports-related destinations, and engaging in adventure sports. By sharing your own sports-related travel experiences and tips, you can provide a unique perspective for sports enthusiasts looking to combine their passions for sports and travel.

In conclusion, this subchapter will equip you with the knowledge and inspiration to create a compelling travel podcast that resonates with your target audience. Whether you are an entrepreneur, business professional, music enthusiast, sports professional, or a film graduate, sharing your travel experiences and tips through podcasting can be an exciting and rewarding venture. So, get ready to embark on a podcasting journey that will transport your listeners to new destinations and inspire them to explore the world.

Exploring Different Cultures through Podcasting

In the digital age, podcasting has become an invaluable tool for connecting with audiences and sharing information. It has allowed individuals from all walks of life to express their thoughts, ideas, and experiences to a global audience. One of the most powerful uses of podcasting is its ability to explore different cultures and bridge the gap between people from diverse backgrounds. In this subchapter, we will dive into the world of cultural podcasting and how it can be a valuable tool for entrepreneurs, business professionals, music professionals, sports enthusiasts, musicians, film graduates, and professionals, as well as individuals interested in personal development, health and wellness, technology and innovation, comedy and entertainment, travel and adventure, and sports.

For entrepreneurs and business professionals, understanding different cultures and their unique practices and perspectives is crucial in today's globalized world. By exploring different cultures through podcasting, they can gain valuable insights into international markets, consumer behaviors, and business trends. This knowledge can help them develop strategic partnerships, expand their customer base, and make informed business decisions.

For music professionals, podcasting provides a platform to discover and showcase music from different cultures. They can interview musicians, share their stories, and expose their work to a wider audience. This not only promotes cultural diversity but also fosters collaboration and cross-pollination of musical styles.

Sports enthusiasts and professionals can also benefit from cultural podcasting. By delving into the sports cultures of different countries, they can gain a deeper understanding of the history, traditions, and values that shape various sports. This knowledge can enhance their appreciation for different sports and drive innovation in their own fields.

Film graduates and professionals can use podcasting as a medium to discuss and analyze films from different cultures. By exploring diverse cinematic experiences, they can broaden their perspectives, discover new storytelling techniques, and gain inspiration for their own projects.

Individuals interested in personal development and self-improvement can find immense value in cultural podcasting. By listening to stories of resilience, perseverance, and personal growth from diverse cultures, they can gain new insights and learn valuable life lessons.

Health and wellness podcasts focused on different cultures can provide listeners with alternative approaches to well-being, traditional healing practices, and holistic lifestyles. This can inspire individuals to adopt healthy habits and explore new wellness techniques.

Technology and innovation podcasts can explore how different cultures embrace and innovate technology. This can lead to the discovery of innovative ideas, strategies, and solutions that can be applied in various industries.

Comedy and entertainment podcasts that embrace cultural diversity can unite people through laughter and humor. By celebrating cultural differences, these podcasts can foster inclusivity, break down stereotypes, and promote understanding.

Podcasts about travel and adventure can transport listeners to different corners of the world, providing them with virtual experiences and inspiring them to explore new destinations.

Podcasts for sports enthusiasts can delve into the rich sports cultures of different countries, sharing captivating stories, and celebrating the passion and dedication of athletes and fans worldwide.

In conclusion, exploring different cultures through podcasting offers entrepreneurs, business professionals, music professionals, sports enthusiasts, musicians, film graduates, and professionals, as well as individuals interested in personal development, health and wellness, technology and innovation, comedy and entertainment, travel and adventure, and sports, a unique opportunity to broaden their horizons, gain new perspectives, and foster meaningful connections. By embracing cultural diversity through podcasting, we can promote understanding, collaboration, and appreciation for the richness that different cultures bring to our world.

Adventure and Outdoor Activities Podcasts

In the fast-paced world of podcasting, there is a genre that stands out for its ability to captivate and inspire listeners from all walks of life – Adventure and Outdoor Activities Podcasts. Whether you are an entrepreneur looking for a breath of fresh air, a business professional seeking inspiration outside the boardroom, or a sports enthusiast yearning for adrenaline-pumping stories, this subchapter explores the best podcasts to fuel your sense of adventure.

For those aspiring entrepreneurs seeking a dose of motivation, podcasts like "The Adventure Zone" and "The Tim Ferriss Show" offer valuable insights into the minds of successful individuals who have followed their passions and built thriving businesses. These podcasts delve into the personal development and self-improvement aspects of entrepreneurship, helping you conquer challenges and embrace the adventurous spirit necessary for success.

If health and wellness are your priorities, podcasts like "The Rich Roll Podcast" and "The Model Health Show" provide valuable information on fitness, nutrition, and mental well-being. These podcasts offer expert advice from professionals in the field, helping you optimize your physical and mental health while embracing the great outdoors.

Technology and innovation enthusiasts will find podcasts like "The Adventure Sports Podcast" and "Outside Podcast" to be a perfect fit. These shows explore the intersection of adventure and technology, showcasing the latest innovations in outdoor gear, apps, and gadgets that enhance your experiences in nature.

For those in need of some laughter and entertainment, podcasts like "The Joe Rogan Experience" and "Conan O'Brien Needs a Friend" offer light-hearted and humorous conversations with celebrities, comedians, and adventurers. These podcasts provide a welcome escape from everyday life and transport you to a world of laughter and entertainment.

Travelers and adventure seekers will be delighted by podcasts such as "Zero To Travel" and "The Dirtbag Diaries." These shows take you on immersive journeys around the world, sharing stories of incredible expeditions, breathtaking landscapes, and life-changing experiences. They provide a window into different cultures and inspire you to embark on your own adventures.

Finally, sports enthusiasts can find their fix in podcasts like "The Bill Simmons Podcast" and "The Ringer NFL Show." These shows dive deep into the world of sports, offering analysis, interviews, and insider information that will keep you engaged and entertained.

No matter your niche or interest, Adventure and Outdoor Activities Podcasts are sure to provide the inspiration, knowledge, and entertainment you seek. So grab your headphones, hit play, and let the adventures unfold.

Inspiring Others to Explore the World

Subchapter: Inspiring Others to Explore the World
In today's fast-paced world, there is an increasing desire among individuals to explore the world, seek new adventures, and broaden their horizons. As a podcaster, you have the unique opportunity to inspire others to embark on their own journeys of exploration and discovery. This subchapter will explore how you can create a podcast that appeals to the innate sense of wanderlust in your audience, while also catering to the diverse interests of

entrepreneurs, business professionals, music professionals, sports enthusiasts, and many more.

Start a podcast in 2024: With the podcasting landscape constantly evolving, it is essential to stay ahead of the curve and start your own podcast in 2024. This subchapter will provide you with a step-by-step guide on how to launch your podcast successfully, including choosing the right niche, selecting the best equipment, and marketing your show effectively.

Podcasts for aspiring entrepreneurs: Aspiring entrepreneurs are always seeking inspiration and guidance from successful individuals in their respective fields. By featuring interviews with business leaders, sharing success stories, and discussing strategies for growth and innovation, your podcast can become a valuable resource for budding entrepreneurs.

Podcasts focused on personal development and self-improvement: Personal development and self-improvement are topics that resonate with a wide range of individuals. By offering actionable advice, motivational stories, and practical tools for personal growth, your podcast can empower listeners to make positive changes in their lives and pursue their dreams.

Health and wellness podcasts: In an increasingly health-conscious society, podcasts focused on health and wellness have gained significant popularity. From fitness tips and nutrition advice to mental health discussions and mindfulness practices, your podcast can inspire listeners to prioritize their well-being and adopt healthier lifestyles.

Technology and innovation podcasts: Technology and innovation shape our world in profound ways. By exploring the latest tech trends, discussing cutting-edge innovations, and interviewing industry experts, your podcast can keep entrepreneurs, business professionals, and tech enthusiasts informed and inspired.

Comedy and entertainment podcasts: Laughter is universal, and comedy podcasts have a broad appeal. By providing light-hearted entertainment, sharing funny anecdotes, and interviewing comedians and entertainers, your podcast can provide a much-needed escape from everyday stress and inspire listeners to embrace joy and laughter.

Podcasts about travel and adventure: Travel and adventure are passions shared by many. By sharing captivating travel stories, providing destination guides, and interviewing globetrotters and explorers, your podcast can ignite the wanderlust in your audience and inspire them to embark on their own extraordinary journeys.

Podcasts for sports enthusiasts: Sports enthusiasts are always hungry for insights, analysis, and behind-the-scenes stories. By covering the latest sports news, interviewing athletes and coaches, and providing in-depth analysis, your podcast can cater to the passion of sports enthusiasts and inspire them to pursue their athletic dreams.

In conclusion, as a podcaster, you have the power to inspire others to explore the world. By creating content that resonates with entrepreneurs, business professionals, music professionals, sports enthusiasts, and more, you can provide a source of motivation, entertainment, and knowledge. So, grab your microphone, embark on your podcasting journey, and inspire others to embrace the wonders of the world.

Chapter 14: Podcasts for Sports Enthusiasts

Analyzing Sports News and Updates Podcasts

Sports news and updates are an integral part of the lives of sports enthusiasts. Whether it's staying updated on the latest scores, player transfers, or game analysis, there is a constant need for reliable and engaging content. Podcasts have emerged as a popular medium for delivering this information, allowing sports enthusiasts to stay connected while on the go. In this subchapter, we will delve into the world of sports news and updates podcasts and explore their significance in the podcasting landscape.

For entrepreneurs and business professionals, sports news and updates podcasts offer valuable insights into the business side of the sports industry. These podcasts often discuss sponsorship deals, marketing strategies, and financial aspects of various sports organizations. By analyzing the trends and decisions made by industry leaders, entrepreneurs can gain valuable knowledge to apply to their own ventures.

Music professionals can also find inspiration in sports news and updates podcasts. These podcasts often feature interviews with athletes, coaches, and sports personalities, offering a unique perspective on success, motivation, and discipline. Musicians can draw parallels between the dedication required in sports and their own creative journeys, finding motivation to push through challenges and achieve their goals.

Film graduates and professionals can benefit from analyzing sports news and updates podcasts as well. These podcasts often provide in-depth analysis of sports events, breaking down game strategies, and discussing memorable moments. By studying the storytelling techniques used in these podcasts, film graduates can gain insights into effective narrative structures, character development, and engaging storytelling.

Sports professionals themselves can also find value in sports news and updates podcasts. These podcasts often feature expert analysis, interviews with coaches and athletes, and discussions on various sports-related topics. By listening to these podcasts, sports professionals can stay up-to-date with the latest industry trends, gain insights from seasoned professionals, and broaden their knowledge base.

Moreover, sports news and updates podcasts cater to a wide range of niche interests. For those interested in personal development and self-improvement, these podcasts often touch upon topics such as leadership, teamwork, and resilience. Health and wellness podcasts within the sports genre can discuss the importance of fitness, nutrition, and mental well-being for athletes.

In conclusion, analyzing sports news and updates podcasts can provide valuable insights and inspiration to a diverse audience. From entrepreneurs and business professionals to sports enthusiasts and musicians, these podcasts offer a wealth of knowledge and entertainment. Whether you're looking to start your own podcast, seeking personal development, or simply staying updated on the latest sports news, exploring this genre is a must for podcast enthusiasts in 2024.

Interviews with Athletes and Sports Professionals

In the world of podcasting, interviews with athletes and sports professionals have become increasingly popular. Not only do these interviews provide valuable insights into the world of sports, but they also offer inspiration and motivation for listeners. Whether you're an entrepreneur, business professional, music enthusiast, or sports professional, this subchapter will explore the benefits of conducting interviews with athletes and sports professionals for your podcast.

For entrepreneurs and business professionals, interviews with athletes and sports professionals can offer valuable lessons in leadership, teamwork, and resilience. Athletes are known for their dedication and discipline, traits that can be applied to any business or entrepreneurial venture. By interviewing successful athletes, you can gain insights into their mindset, strategies for success, and lessons learned from their journey. These interviews can serve as a source of inspiration for aspiring entrepreneurs, providing them with the motivation to pursue their dreams and overcome obstacles.

For music professionals and film graduates, interviews with athletes and sports professionals can offer a unique perspective on the creative process. Athletes, like musicians and filmmakers, often have to push themselves to their limits and think outside the box to achieve greatness. By interviewing athletes, you can explore the parallels between the worlds of sports and entertainment, uncovering the similarities in their creative processes and the challenges they face.

Sports enthusiasts and professionals can benefit from interviews with athletes and sports professionals by gaining a deeper understanding of their favorite sports and athletes. These interviews can provide behind-the-scenes insights, training tips, and personal stories that can enhance their appreciation for the sport. Whether you're a fan of football, basketball, soccer, or any other sport, interviews with athletes and sports professionals can offer a unique perspective and a deeper connection to the sports world.

In conclusion, interviews with athletes and sports professionals can be a valuable addition to any podcast. They offer inspiration, motivation, and insights into the world of sports that can benefit entrepreneurs, business professionals, music enthusiasts, film graduates, and sports enthusiasts alike. Whether you're interested in personal development, health and wellness, technology and innovation, comedy and entertainment, or travel and adventure, interviews with athletes and sports professionals have something to offer.

So, why wait? Start incorporating interviews with athletes and sports professionals into your podcast today and take your content to the next level.

Fantasy Sports and Betting Podcasts

In recent years, the popularity of fantasy sports and sports betting has skyrocketed. Fans are no longer content with simply watching their favorite teams and players; they want to be actively involved in the game. This has given rise to a new breed of podcasts dedicated to fantasy sports and betting, providing enthusiasts with insights, analysis, and tips to gain the edge in their competitions.

For entrepreneurs and business professionals looking to tap into the podcasting industry, starting a podcast focused on fantasy sports and betting could be a lucrative endeavor. The growing interest in this niche presents a unique opportunity to engage with an enthusiastic and dedicated audience. By offering valuable content and expert advice, you can establish yourself as an authority in the field and attract a loyal following.

Aspiring entrepreneurs can also benefit from fantasy sports and betting podcasts. These podcasts can provide valuable lessons in strategy, risk assessment, and decision-making, which are essential skills for any business venture. By listening to interviews with industry experts, analyzing their methods, and applying their insights to your own endeavors, you can gain valuable knowledge and inspiration to enhance your entrepreneurial journey.

Personal development and self-improvement are topics that resonate with a wide audience. Fantasy sports and betting podcasts offer a unique twist on personal growth by incorporating elements of strategy, analysis, and critical thinking. By tuning in to these podcasts, listeners can learn how to make informed decisions, manage risk, and adapt to changing circumstances – skills that are valuable not only in sports but also in their personal and professional lives.

Health and wellness are important aspects of any individual's life. While fantasy sports and betting may not directly relate to physical fitness, these podcasts can provide an escape from daily stresses and offer a form of entertainment that promotes mental agility and engagement. By taking a break from the rigors of daily life and indulging in the excitement of fantasy sports and betting, listeners can enjoy a mental workout that keeps their minds sharp and active.

Technology and innovation are constantly shaping the world we live in. Fantasy sports and betting podcasts often explore the latest advancements in data analytics, artificial intelligence, and predictive modeling. By keeping up with these trends, sports enthusiasts can gain a deeper understanding of the tools and techniques used in the industry. This knowledge can be applied to other areas of interest, making these podcasts relevant even for those outside of the sports world.

Comedy and entertainment are integral to the podcasting landscape. Fantasy sports and betting podcasts provide a unique blend of informative analysis and lighthearted banter, creating an enjoyable listening experience. The hosts' wit, humor, and camaraderie make these podcasts engaging and entertaining for sports enthusiasts and casual listeners alike.

For those who crave adventure and exploration, fantasy sports and betting podcasts can transport them to the thrilling world of sports competitions. These podcasts often delve into the intricacies of different sports, offering insights into players, teams, and game strategies. Listeners can immerse themselves in the excitement of the game, even if they are not physically present at the event.

Lastly, sports enthusiasts can find a wealth of content tailored to their interests in fantasy sports and betting podcasts. From in-depth analysis of players' performances to discussions on game predictions and betting strategies, these podcasts cater to the passionate fan base. By tuning in, sports enthusiasts can stay up to date with the latest news, insights, and trends in their favorite sports.

In conclusion, fantasy sports and betting podcasts offer a diverse range of content that appeals to entrepreneurs, business professionals, music professionals, sports enthusiasts, sports professionals, musicians, film graduates, and film professionals. Whether you are looking to start a podcast, gain entrepreneurial insights, improve personal development, enhance health and wellness, explore technology and innovation, seek entertainment, embark on travel and adventure, or indulge in sports-related discussions, fantasy sports and betting podcasts provide a comprehensive and engaging listening experience.

Engaging with Sports Fan Communities

In the world of podcasting, engaging with sports fan communities can be a game-changer for your show. Whether you're a sports enthusiast yourself or simply targeting a niche audience, tapping into the passion and dedication of sports fans can take your podcast to new heights. In this subchapter, we'll explore strategies to connect with sports fan communities and create content that resonates with this enthusiastic audience.

Understanding the Sports Fan Mindset

Sports fans are a unique breed, characterized by their unwavering loyalty and emotional investment in their favorite teams and athletes.

To truly engage with this community, you must understand their mindset and speak their language. Research the history, culture, and traditions associated with the sports you'll be discussing on your podcast. This will allow you to connect with fans on a deeper level and earn their trust.

Guest Interviews and Expert Analysis

One effective way to engage with sports fan communities is by bringing in guest interviews and expert analysis. Reach out to athletes, coaches, sports journalists, and industry insiders to offer their insights and perspectives. This not only adds credibility to your show but also gives fans exclusive access to their favorite sports figures. Encourage your audience to submit questions or topics they'd like to hear discussed, further involving them in the conversation.

Interactive Social Media Presence

Sports fans are active on social media platforms, making it essential to have a strong presence there. Create engaging content like polls, quizzes, and fan debates to encourage interaction and foster a sense of community. Respond promptly to comments and messages, and show genuine interest in your audience's opinions. This will not only help you build a loyal fan base but also provide valuable insights for future podcast episodes.

Live Events and Fan Meetups

Consider organizing live events and fan meetups to connect with your audience in person. Whether it's hosting a tailgate party before a big game or organizing a sports-themed trivia night, these events create memorable experiences and strengthen the bond between your podcast and its fans. Collaborate with local businesses and sports venues to make these events a success.

Consistency and Authenticity

Lastly, be consistent with your podcast episodes and maintain an authentic voice throughout. Sports fans appreciate regular updates and crave genuine discussions. Stay true to your brand and provide content that is both informative and entertaining. By consistently delivering high-quality episodes and engaging with your audience, you'll establish your podcast as a trusted source for sports-related content.

Engaging with sports fan communities is an exciting opportunity to connect with a passionate audience. By understanding the sports fan mindset, incorporating guest interviews and expert analysis, utilizing social media, organizing live events, and staying consistent and authentic, your podcast will become a go-to resource for sports enthusiasts seeking engaging and informative content.

Chapter 15: Conclusion and Future of Podcasting

Reflecting on Your Podcasting Journey

Congratulations! By this point, you have embarked on an incredible journey as a podcaster. In this subchapter, we will delve into the importance of reflecting on your podcasting journey. Whether you are an entrepreneur, business professional, musician, film graduate, or sports enthusiast, reflecting on your podcasting experience is crucial for growth and improvement.

Starting a podcast in 2024 has opened up a world of possibilities for you. It has given you a platform to share your expertise, passions, and stories with a global audience. As you reflect on your podcasting journey, take a moment to appreciate how far you have come.

Remember the excitement that sparked your interest and the determination that fueled your progress.

Podcasts for aspiring entrepreneurs have the power to inspire and educate. Reflect on how your podcast has impacted the entrepreneurial community. Have you shared valuable insights, interviewed successful entrepreneurs, or provided practical advice? Consider the feedback you have received and identify areas for improvement. Reflecting on your podcasting journey can help you refine your content, deliver more value, and attract a larger audience.

For those focused on personal development and self-improvement, your podcast has the potential to be a catalyst for change. Reflect on the topics you have covered and the impact they have had on your listeners. Have you helped them set goals, develop new habits, or overcome challenges? Consider the testimonials and messages of gratitude you have received. Reflecting on your podcasting journey can help you continue to provide content that empowers and motivates your audience.

Health and wellness podcasts have become increasingly popular in recent years. As you reflect on your podcasting journey in this niche, consider the impact you have had on your listeners' lives. Have you provided valuable information, shared inspiring stories, or given practical advice for maintaining a healthy lifestyle? Reflecting on your podcasting journey can help you tailor your content to address the specific needs and interests of your audience.

Technology and innovation podcasts have the ability to shape the future. As a podcaster in this niche, reflect on the topics you have explored and the conversations you have sparked. Have you interviewed industry experts, discussed emerging technologies, or predicted future trends? Consider the impact your podcast has had on your listeners' understanding and awareness of technology and innovation. Reflecting on your podcasting journey can help you stay ahead of the curve and continue to provide valuable insights.

Comedy and entertainment podcasts have the power to bring joy and laughter to millions. As you reflect on your podcasting journey in this niche, consider the moments of pure entertainment you have created. Have you shared hilarious stories, interviewed comedians, or discussed trending topics in the entertainment industry? Reflecting on your podcasting journey can help you refine your comedic style, engage your audience, and create memorable content.

Podcasts about travel and adventure have the ability to transport listeners to far-off places and inspire them to explore the world. As you reflect on your podcasting journey in this niche, consider the stories you have shared and the destinations you have uncovered. Have you provided travel tips, interviewed adventurers, or shared personal experiences? Reflecting on your podcasting journey can help you continue to ignite the wanderlust in your listeners and provide valuable insights for their own adventures.

For sports enthusiasts, your podcast has become a hub for news, analysis, and discussions. As you reflect on your podcasting journey in this niche, consider the impact you have had on your audience's understanding and enjoyment of sports. Have you provided in-depth analysis, interviewed athletes, or shared captivating stories? Reflecting on your podcasting journey can help you stay up to date with the latest sports news, engage your audience, and provide unique perspectives.

In conclusion, reflecting on your podcasting journey is a vital step in your growth as a podcaster. Whether you are an entrepreneur, business professional, musician, film graduate, or sports enthusiast, taking the time to reflect can help you refine your content, engage your audience, and continue to provide value. Embrace the lessons learned, celebrate your successes, and let your podcasting journey inspire you to reach new heights in the ever-evolving world of podcasting.

(Note: The content provided here is a sample and should be used for reference purposes only.)

Embracing the Evolving Podcasting Landscape

As we venture into the year 2024, the podcasting landscape continues to evolve at a rapid pace. With millions of podcasts available for listeners, it is crucial for entrepreneurs, business professionals, music professionals, sports enthusiasts, musicians, film graduates, and professionals to embrace these changes and stay ahead of the game. In this subchapter, we will explore the key trends and opportunities in podcasting, catering to various niches and interests.

Start a podcast in 2024:

Starting a podcast has never been easier, and 2024 is the perfect time to jump on the bandwagon. With the increasing popularity and accessibility of podcasting platforms, now is the time to unleash your creativity and share your unique voice with the world. We will guide you through the step-by-step process of launching your podcast, from choosing the right equipment and software to marketing and monetization strategies.

Podcasts for aspiring entrepreneurs:

For entrepreneurs looking to gain an edge in the competitive business world, podcasts offer a wealth of knowledge and inspiration. We will explore podcasts that feature interviews with successful entrepreneurs, providing valuable insights into their journeys, strategies, and lessons learned. These podcasts will equip you with the necessary tools to navigate the challenges of entrepreneurship and achieve your goals.

Podcasts focused on personal development and self-improvement:
In a fast-paced world, personal development and self-improvement
have become essential. We will delve into podcasts that offer
practical tips and advice on topics such as mindfulness, productivity,
motivation, and overcoming obstacles. Discover podcasts that will
empower you to become the best version of yourself and unlock
your true potential.

Health and wellness podcasts:
As the importance of health and wellness gains traction, podcasts
dedicated to these topics have seen a surge in popularity. From
nutrition and fitness to mental health and holistic healing, we will
explore podcasts that provide expert advice, interviews with
healthcare professionals, and personal stories that inspire positive
lifestyle changes.

Technology and innovation podcasts:
Innovation drives progress, and technology plays a pivotal role in
shaping our future. We will showcase podcasts that explore the latest
technological advancements, trends, and their impact on various
industries. Stay informed and inspired by discussions with tech
experts, entrepreneurs, and thought leaders.

Comedy and entertainment podcasts:
Laughter is the best medicine, and the world of comedy podcasts
offers a limitless source of entertainment. We will introduce you to
podcasts featuring stand-up comedians, improv shows, and comedic
storytelling. Tune in and let the laughter boost your mood and
brighten your day.

Podcasts about travel and adventure:
For wanderlust enthusiasts seeking inspiration and travel tips,
podcasts have become an invaluable resource. We will highlight
podcasts that feature travel stories, destination guides, and interviews
with seasoned travelers. Embark on virtual journeys and let these
podcasts fuel your sense of adventure.

Podcasts for sports enthusiasts:

Sports lovers can now enjoy podcasts that provide in-depth analysis, interviews with athletes, and discussions on the latest sporting events. Whether you're a fan of football, basketball, tennis, or any other sport, we will guide you to podcasts that cater to your specific interests. Stay up to date with the latest news and insights from the sporting world.

In conclusion, the podcasting landscape in 2024 offers a plethora of opportunities for entrepreneurs, business professionals, music professionals, sports enthusiasts, musicians, film graduates, and professionals alike. By embracing these changes and exploring podcasts tailored to your interests, you can stay informed, inspired, and entertained in this ever-evolving industry.

Predictions for the Future of Podcasting in 2024 and Beyond

As we look ahead to the future of podcasting, it is clear that this medium is set to continue its exponential growth and influence in various industries. In this subchapter, we will explore some exciting predictions for the future of podcasting in 2024 and beyond, catering to the diverse interests of our audience, including entrepreneurs, business professionals, music professionals, sports enthusiasts, sports professionals, musicians, film graduates, film professionals, and more.

Start a podcast in 2024:

With the increasing accessibility of podcasting tools and platforms, starting a podcast will become even easier in the coming years. Improved technology and user-friendly interfaces will empower aspiring podcasters to share their stories, ideas, and expertise with the world. The podcasting landscape will become more competitive, prompting podcasters to focus on unique content and innovative strategies to stand out from the crowd.

Podcasts for aspiring entrepreneurs:

In 2024, podcasts dedicated to entrepreneurship will flourish. These podcasts will offer valuable insights, interviews with successful entrepreneurs, and practical tips for starting and scaling businesses. Aspiring entrepreneurs will find guidance, inspiration, and a supportive community through these podcasts, helping them navigate the challenges and triumphs of their entrepreneurial journey.

Podcasts focused on personal development and self-improvement:

In an era where personal growth and self-improvement are highly valued, podcasts centered around these themes will continue to thrive. Experts in psychology, motivation, mindfulness, and productivity will deliver valuable content, helping listeners enhance their well-being, achieve their goals, and unlock their full potential.

Health and wellness podcasts:

With the increasing awareness of health and wellness, podcasts dedicated to these topics will become more prevalent. In 2024, we can expect a surge in podcasts covering nutrition, fitness, mental health, alternative therapies, and holistic well-being. These podcasts will serve as a valuable resource for individuals seeking to prioritize their health and make informed lifestyle choices.

Technology and innovation podcasts:

As technology continues to evolve, so will the demand for podcasts exploring the latest trends and innovations. In 2024, technology-focused podcasts will delve into emerging technologies such as artificial intelligence, blockchain, virtual reality, and more. These podcasts will provide valuable insights into the future of technology, inspiring entrepreneurs and professionals in various industries to adapt and innovate.

Comedy and entertainment podcasts:

Laughter will never go out of style, and comedy podcasts will remain a popular genre in the podcasting world. In 2024, we can expect an influx of comedy and entertainment podcasts, offering a much-needed escape from the stresses of daily life. Whether through hilarious storytelling, improv, or interviews with comedians, these podcasts will continue to bring joy and entertainment to listeners worldwide.

Podcasts about travel and adventure:

For the wanderlust-driven individuals, travel and adventure podcasts will be a go-to source for inspiration and practical advice. In 2024, we anticipate an increase in podcasts dedicated to exploring different destinations, sharing travel hacks, and providing insights into unique cultural experiences. These podcasts will fuel the sense of adventure and ignite the desire to explore the world.

Podcasts for sports enthusiasts:

Sports enthusiasts will have an abundance of podcasts to choose from in 2024. From in-depth analysis of sporting events, interviews with athletes, and discussions on sports psychology and performance, these podcasts will cater to the insatiable appetite of sports fans. Whether you're a die-hard fan or a sports professional, these podcasts will keep you informed and engaged.

In conclusion, the future of podcasting is bright and promising. As the medium continues to evolve, entrepreneurs, business professionals, music professionals, sports enthusiasts, musicians, film professionals, and individuals from various backgrounds will find an array of podcasting content that caters to their unique interests and passions. Whether it's starting a podcast, seeking personal growth, staying informed about the latest technology, or finding entertainment, podcasts will continue to be an invaluable source of knowledge, inspiration, and entertainment in 2024 and beyond.

Inspiring Others to Start Their Own Podcasts

Podcasting has become an incredibly popular medium in recent years, with millions of people around the world tuning in to listen to their favorite shows. If you're an entrepreneur, business professional, music enthusiast, sports professional, or anyone looking to share their knowledge and experiences, starting your own podcast could be a game-changer for you.

In this subchapter, we will explore the various ways you can inspire others to start their own podcasts. Whether you're passionate about personal development, health and wellness, technology and innovation, comedy and entertainment, or sports, there's a niche for everyone in the podcasting world. Let's dive in and discover how you can motivate others to embark on this exciting journey.

One of the most effective ways to inspire others is by sharing your own success story. As a podcast host, you have a unique platform to showcase your expertise and experiences, demonstrating how podcasting has transformed your life and career. By highlighting the benefits and opportunities that come with podcasting, you can ignite curiosity and spark interest in others who may be considering starting their own show.

Another powerful strategy is to feature successful podcasters and industry experts as guests on your show. By inviting these individuals to share their insights and stories, you not only provide valuable content for your listeners but also inspire aspiring podcasters to take the leap. Hearing firsthand how others have overcome challenges, built a loyal audience, and found success through podcasting can be incredibly motivating.

Additionally, hosting workshops or webinars focused on podcasting can be a great way to inspire others. These interactive sessions allow you to share your knowledge and expertise, providing practical tips and guidance on how to get started. By offering support and guidance, you can help aspiring podcasters navigate the initial hurdles and set them on the path to success.

Lastly, leveraging social media platforms and online communities can greatly expand your reach and inspire others. Share snippets of your podcast episodes, engage with your audience, and encourage discussions around podcasting topics. By building a community of like-minded individuals, you create a space for aspiring podcasters to connect, share ideas, and find inspiration.

In conclusion, inspiring others to start their own podcasts is an essential part of fostering a vibrant and diverse podcasting community. By sharing your own experiences, featuring industry experts, hosting workshops, and leveraging social media, you can motivate entrepreneurs, business professionals, music enthusiasts, sports professionals, and individuals from various niches to embark on their podcasting journey. So, let's create a world where everyone's voice can be heard, and ideas can flourish through the power of podcasting.

www.ingramcontent.com/pod-product-compliance
Lightning Source LLC
LaVergne TN
LVHW051703050326
832903LV00032B/3980